NINE ULSTER LIVES

NINE ULSTER LIVES

EDITED BY

G. O'BRIEN & P. ROEBUCK

THE ULSTER HISTORICAL FOUNDATION

FRONT COVER ILLUSTRATIONS FROM TOP ARE —

Claude Auchinleck; painting by R.G. Eves, 1940
Courtesy the National Portrait Gallery

Detail: Portrait of William Paterson by Mrs B.S. Church
Courtesy The Art Museum, Princeton University

Helen Waddell; painting by Grace Henry
Courtesy Miss Molly Martin

BACK COVER ILLUSTRATIONS CLOCKWISE ARE —

Owen Roe O'Neill; painting anonymous
Courtesy the Trustees of the Ulster Museum

John Abernethy; mezzotint by Latham/Brooks
Courtesy the National Gallery of Ireland

Charles Gavan Duffy; lithograph by Gluckman/O'Neill
Courtesy the National Gallery of Ireland

Ernest Walton; photograph by New Pics
Courtesy the National Portrait Gallery

John Dunlap; owner of original unknown
Copy kindly provided by the Ulster American Folk Park

John Lavery; self portrait, 1928
Courtesy the Trustees of the Ulster Museum

Published 1992
by the Ulster Historical Foundation
12 College Square East, Belfast, BT16DD

ISBN 0 901 905 51 8
Typesetting by the Ulster Historical Foundation
Printed by the Universities Press (Belfast) Ltd
Alanbrooke Road, Belfast, BT6 9HF

This book has received support from the Cultural Traditions Programme
of the Community Relations Council which aims to encourage
acceptance and understanding of cultural diversity.

Design by Wendy Dunbar

CONTENTS

INTRODUCTION 7

ERNEST WALTON 13

1903- Atomic Scientist, *Brian Cathcart*

CLAUDE AUCHINLECK 33

1884–1981 Military Leader, *Thomas G. Fraser*

HELEN WADDELL 55

1889–1965 Scholar and Author, *Felicitas Corrigan*

JOHN LAVERY 73

1856–1941 Painter, *Kenneth McConkey*

CHARLES GAVAN DUFFY 87

1816–1903 Rebel and Statesman, *Gerard O' Brien*

JOHN DUNLAP 99

c.1746–1812 Printer, *Roy McCaughey*

WILLIAM PATERSON 111

1745–1806 Lawyer and Politician, *Steve Ickringill*

JOHN ABERNETHY 125

1680–1740 Scholar and Ecclesiast, *A. Godfrey Brown*

OWEN ROE O'NEILL 149

c.1582–1649 Soldier and Politician, *Raymond Gillespie*

NOTES AND REFERENCES 167

ACKNOWLEDGEMENTS

The Editors and the Ulster Historical Foundation wish to acknowledge the following for permission to reproduce illustrations: Photograph of Ernest Walton, p. 14, used by courtesy of the National Portrait Gallery London; painting of Helen Waddell, p. 34, by Grace Henry, reproduced by courtesy of Miss Molly Martin; painting of Claude Auchinleck, p. 52, by R.G. Eves, by courtesy of the National Portrait Gallery, London; photograph of John Lavery, p. 74, supplied by Kenneth McConkey; lithograph of Charles Gavan Duffy, p. 88, by Gluckman/O'Neill, by courtesy of the National Gallery of Ireland; portrait of John Dunlap, p. 100, copy provided by the Ulster American Folk Park. Whilst every effort was made to trace the owner of the original of this portrait, the search proved unsuccessful. We will happily acknowledge the owner in any future edition if we can locate them. Portrait of William Paterson, p. 112, by Mrs B.S. Church, by courtesy of the Art Museum, Princeton University; mezzotint of John Abernethy, p. 126, by Latham/Brooks, by courtesy of the National Gallery of Ireland; portrait of Owen Roe O'Neill, p. 150, anonymous, by kind permission of the Ulster Museum.

The following individuals provided invaluable help in tracing illustrations: Christine McIvor at the Ulster American Folk Park, Bonnie Kaplan at Rutgers University Press, Richard P. McCormick, Karen Richter at the Art Museum, Princeton University, Vivienne Pollack at the Ulster Museum, Miss Molly Martin and Wendy Dunbar. Thanks are also due to Mr George Brittain of Brittain Laboratories for help in preparing the text for the printers.

INTRODUCTION

Few Ulster persons, irrespective of their political leanings, would disagree that endurance is a central feature of the northern Irish character. Only a handful of latter-day societies can boast (if that is the word) of political cultures so steadfast in their survival of the centuries that they find fresh and renewed vibrance in an environment foreign in every way to that which first nurtured them. One of the perhaps inevitable consequences of the current strife in Ulster is that the more positive elements in the Ulster character have been forgotten. The contemporary world has been conditioned to associate the region only with the collective nadir of anti-social behaviour and attitudes.

This volume of essays originated in the clear need to remind outside commentators as well as more localised cynics that innumerable Ulstermen and women have made great and lasting contributions to modern civilization. Moreover, it was not designed as a purely academic exercise. The contributors are united in a clear appreciation of the need for works of history which are accessible to the general public. The writing of Ulster history, as indeed of any history, cannot flourish in isolation from the local community. The figures portrayed in this book are remembered by history for their personal attributes and their public roles. Few are remembered (except perhaps by obituarists) as having been born or bred in Ulster, and certainly none has been credited with having imbibed the characteristics which helped to make their fame from their northern Irish roots. But this 'de-Ulsterized' view the world has adopted of quintessential Ulster persons does not reflect merely ignorance or prejudice. In part it stems from the varying appreciation by the persons themselves of their Ulster heritage. It is a fact that while the environment of birth and upbringing is a formative influence, other influences — particularly those experienced in the wider world outside Ulster — may be equally or even more formative. Some of the central characters of this book carried with them a warm appreciation of their Ulster background, and a few returned to their roots to visit or to remain as their lives drew to a close. Others sustained the 'Ulster' side of their identity silently and in a few cases, perhaps even unsuspectingly, revealed their unique inherited qualities only at infrequent but critical intervals. If these latter are the hardest to detect, their discovery is correspondingly the more rewarding.

No attempt has been made to persuade individual authors to highlight Ulster traits or behaviour patterns in the lives of their subjects. Some of the authors share an Ulster background with their subjects, and some do not. Whereas many persons, authors and readers, would hold common views on what constitutes a definitively Ulster characteristic, few would be in agreement on all such alleged traits. Some, perhaps not unjustifiably, would see racialist or political innuendo within such propositions, and be offended accordingly. Therefore, it has been decided to exclude all such detective work and to allow the authors to tell their subjects' stories as they see fit, and to leave the implications where they may fall.

To some extent the selection of subjects has been defined by practicalities. There were very many Ulstermen and women who would have fitted perfectly the biographical parameters intended by the planners of this volume, but only nine could be included. The nine listed here were not selected with any arbitrary intention to present a balance of figures from latter-day nationalists and loyalist communities. Many of the subjects were unconnected or unconcerned with politics, past or present, and their memory would have been ill-served by making them part of an argument to which their lives had no genuine relevance. The balance sought was to indicate the Ulster contribution in as many walks of life as possible within the nine-life limit and, by adopting a deliberate historical standpoint, to illustrate this contribution over the centuries. In this we have not been entirely successful. When an Ulster economist of sufficient standing was found, no author could be matched to him. Some Ulstermen left their fame behind them but not their papers. Sometimes subjects, and even authors, had to be dispensed with in order that an imbalance of periods did not emerge. In the final analysis the nine are composed of one seventeenth-century military leader (O'Neill); one seventeenth/eighteenth-century clergyman (Abernethy); two eighteenth-century Irish-American colonists (Paterson and Dunlap); one nineteenth-century statesman (Duffy); a painter (Lavery), a military leader (Auchinleck), and a literary figure (Waddell) from the nineteenth/twentieth centures; and one, Ernest Walton, a twentieth-century man still living.

It would not do to anticipate the content of each essay, but a few words on each of the subjects may serve to whet the appetite. Born in 1903 and educated in Belfast, Dublin and Cambridge, Ernest Walton played a part of central significance in early atomic energy experiments. He was awarded the Nobel Prize for Physics (with Sir John Cockcroft) in 1951, and now lives in retirement in Dublin. Helen Waddell, born in 1889 and educated in Belfast, is best known through her many scholarly works. These include *The Wandering Scholars* and *Peter Abelard* which have gone through many editions. She was one of the leading figures of a literary community illuminated by Shaw, Sassoon and Russell. Helen died in 1965. Claude Auchinleck was born in 1884. An army careerist from a soldier's family, he served in the Middle East during the First World War, and later in India. He is remembered principally, and perhaps with less than justice, for his crucial role in halting the advance of Rommel during the desert campaign of 1942. The final part of Auchinleck's career was spent in India where he was Commander-in-Chief during the transition to independence.

John Lavery was born in Belfast and studied art in Glasgow, London and Paris. Success came early with his representation of

Queen Victoria's visit to the Glasgow Exhibition in 1888. Following a long and distinguished career, perhaps most memorably in portraiture, he died in Kilkenny in 1941. Charles Gavan Duffy (1816-1903) lived the parts of Irish rebel, Australian statesman and historian. His strange ability to fuse in his broad identity phenomena such as journalism and nationalism, legal skills and constitutionalism, imperialism and popular rights makes him one of Victorian Ireland's most memorable figures.

In a sense William Paterson and John Dunlap grew up with the American Revolution. Dunlap's origins are shadowy, but Paterson is known to have been born in Antrim in 1745, a year or two before Dunlap. Dunlap is remembered mainly as the printer of the Declaration of Independenece. Dr McCaughey fleshes out this sketch to reveal a committed militiaman and entrepreneur who died prosperous and contented in 1812. Paterson played no less a distinguished part in the creation of post-colonial America, being the first Attorney General of New Jersey and a controversial figure at the Philadelphia Convention of 1787. He died in 1806, heavy with honours bestowed by a grateful nation.

John Abernethy (1680-1740), a Presbyterian clergyman of outstanding scholarship, was ordained in Antrim. His determination to return there after being sent to Dublin by his Synod led to a split in the Presbyterian Church and to the eventual emergence of Unitarians — 'the non-subscribers' who had taken Abernethy's side in the affair. No stranger to controversy, he entered into debate with the great Swift and was one of the foremost opponents of the Test Act. His prodigious outpourings were ended only by his death in 1740. Born about 1590 and deprived of his patrimony through his uncle's flight from Ireland, Owen Roe O'Neill followed a distinguished career in the Spanish army. His return to Ireland in 1642 gave direction and greater purpose to the on-going Ulster rebellion (which had broken out the previous October). O'Neill adopted Royalist and Catholic credentials, and under his leadership the Irish achieved their only significant military triumph — the defeat of Monroe's forces at Benburb in 1646. His day, however, was brief; he fell ill during the autumn of 1649 and died on 6 November.

It remains only to thank the various individuals and bodies whose inspiration, perseverence and patience have made this book possible. Principally they are Brian Trainor and the members of the Ulster Historical Foundation who helped to give it proper balance and coherence; and Christine Kinealy, Trevor Parkhill, John Walsh and Joe Passmore who bore the brunt of the administrative work connected with the book. To all of them the editors and contributors extend their grateful thanks.

ERNEST WALTON

1903–

Atomic Scientist

Brian Cathcart

ERNEST WALTON

At the end of April 1932 a short letter, five paragraphs in length, appeared in the London scientific journal *Nature*. Beneath the headline 'Disintegration of Lithium by Swift Protons', the authors revealed that, employing high voltages, they had bombarded atoms of the element lithium with lesser particles called protons. The result was that some lithium atoms absorbed the protons and then divided in two, releasing as they did so a certain amount of energy. 'Experiments are in progress', the letter concluded, 'to determine the effect on other elements when bombarded by a stream of swift protons and other particles.'[1]

By this unspectacular communication the world was informed of one of the great scientific advances of the century. The letter was signed by two men: John Cockcroft, a Lancashire mill-owner's son who had come to university physics research after service in the Great War and a spell in the engineering industry; and Ernest Walton, son of an Irish clergyman, former pupil of Methodist College, Belfast and graduate of Trinity College, Dublin. Their letter caused a sensation, for what it announced, in layman's terms, was that man could now split the atom at will. 'Wonderful new results', exclaimed Niels Bohr, one of the outstanding theoreticians of the time, who wrote from Denmark to express his 'very great pleasure'.[2] Across the Atlantic, the experimental physicist Ernest Lawrence interrupted his honeymoon on hearing the news and cabled California to tell his colleagues to try the experiment. Soon he too sent his congratulations. Cockcroft and Walton were the toast of the physics world.

In the wider world as well, they were famous. Their announcement coincided with the opening in the West End of a play called

Wings over Europe, which told the story of a scientist who gains control of the energy in the atom. After turning a key into rubber and causing a large explosion with a sugar-lump, he holds the world to ransom. 'Where this island was,' he warns the British Cabinet, 'will be a whirlpool of disintegrating atoms.'[3] He is shot, however, and the world is saved. This coincidence of fiction with fact helped to promote the little letter in *Nature* into a story in the national press. Journalists hurried to Cambridge to find the two scientists and their atom-splitting apparatus. Any who hoped to see a key turned to rubber or a sugar-lump explode were disappointed, but they found consolation when it was explained that the ungainly machine in the Cavendish Laboratory did indeed change one element into another, albeit in infinitesimally small quantities. It may not have been base metal into gold, but it could be called a sort of alchemy.

Cockcroft and Walton were to share the Nobel prize, and Walton remains the only Irish scientist, from north or south, to have been so honoured. It was characteristic of the man that, upon learning of the award, he declared himself 'the most surprised person in the country'.[4]

Ernest Thomas Sinton Walton was born on 6 October 1903 in Dungarvan, Co. Waterford. His father, John, was a Limerick man, the son of a shopkeeper, while his mother, Anna, was from an old Co. Armagh family, the Sintons. They had met and married when John was the local minister in the Armagh town of Richhill. The Methodist Church had at that time a rule that its ministers should stay no more than three years in one parish, so the young couple soon left Richhill, first for Dungarvan and then for Rathkeale in Co. Limerick, where Anna died, leaving John with a son, Ernest, and a daughter.

For the children, a peripatetic life was just beginning, although henceforth their family home was always in Ulster — Banbridge, Cookstown, Tanderagee, Lurgan, Glenavy and Coleraine. In Ulster, Ernest enjoyed a happy childhood, received a first-class schooling and acquired an accent that was to stay with him all his life. For his father, the ministries in the North were more of a challenge than they might have been, since he was a Home Ruler and most of his parishioners were not. John Walton was not one to hide his views. When in 1912, at the height of the Home Rule crisis, local Unionists in Cookstown came to his church and suggested placing the loyalist Covenant in the porch on Sunday for supporters to sign, he sent them packing. Ernest briefly attended schools in Banbridge and Cookstown but in 1915 he was sent as a boarder to Methody in Belfast, where his father had been a pupil before him. There he spent seven fulfilling years and, into the bargain, met the girl who was to become his wife.

In more than one sense, the scientist was already taking shape in the Belfast schoolboy of those wartime years. From his father, an amateur astronomer, he inherited a curiosity about the workings of the natural world, while even as a child he exhibited a gift for making things with his hands — carpentry tools were a usual birthday present. At Methody, enthusiastic science and mathematics teachers nurtured his talents, occasionally at the expense of other subjects. French, for example, held no attraction for him and, much later, he recalled handing in some rather poor French homework. 'I know what happened last night', said the teacher. 'You spent all your time working on maths for Mr Lloyd and when you were tired you did your French.' This was wrong, but the young pupil did not dare tell the truth: that he had rushed off the French so he could do his maths at leisure.

The teachers he admired were graduates of Trinity College, Dublin, as was his father; when the time came, Ernest decided to go there too. For this, money had to be found, and that was no simple matter. He put his name down to compete for a Trinity award called a sizarship, which would pay his fees and provide dinner — Commons - every evening. In addition, he applied for one of the £40-a-year scholarships being offered by each county of the new state of Northern Ireland. These carried two requirements: five years' residence in the county and a good mark in the Queen's University entrance exam. By chance, John Walton had served consecutive parishes in Armagh, so Ernest could declare himself an Armagh man. That left him with two sets of examinations to sit.

The Trinity exams occurred during a break in the Queen's exams, but when Walton turned up at Great Victoria Street station in Belfast to take a train to Dublin, he found that services had been cancelled because civil war had broken out in the south. Sharing his predicament, he discovered, was a young man from Ballymena called A. J. McConnell. It was fortunate for Trinity that they were given another chance to sit the exams, for not only was Walton to bring the university great honour, but McConnell became one of its most distinguished Provosts. Examinations never seem to have caused the young Ernest any difficulty. Like all good students, he studied the papers of previous years, the better to prepare himself. In the case of the Trinity sizarship, this led him to choose mathematics instead of science; the science standard was so low that he suspected most candidates would score high marks and he feared that his untidy handwriting would then count against him! He duly won his sizarship and entered university, the world that was to be his for the rest of his long career.

Trinity in the 1920s was, by all accounts, an agreeable place. When Walton arrived the Civil War was not yet over; students were occasionally searched for arms on Grafton Street and the sound of gunfire sometimes drifted over Front Square, but the College itself was an insulated and contented community. Walton took rooms on campus with a cousin, dined on Commons every night, ran with the Harriers on Saturdays and, in summer, played a little tennis. He also worked hard and was usually top of his class in both mathematics and physics, although A. J. McConnell provided stiff competition in the former.

While Trinity's standards in mathematics at that time were high, those in physics were not. 'Looking at the course of lectures as a whole', Walton has written, 'I think it can be fairly described as an up-to-date one for about the year 1910.'[5] This was 1922. The core of the physics staff was the Thrift brothers, W. E. and Harry. The former, who was the professor, was unable to keep order in lectures and had to rely on the latter, a former rugby international, to instil respect in his students. Under this regime, one history of the university declares, 'the department can best be described as stagnant'.[6] Walton's interest in the subject nonetheless flourished, although he did not commit himself firmly to physics rather than maths until after he had graduated in 1926, when he embarked upon an M.Sc. Then it was his love of making things that tipped the balance: experimental physics offered him the chance to design and build apparatus, and he knew that good maths would always be an asset. While working for his M.Sc., Walton found that he might qualify for a British '1851 Exhibition' scholarship to pursue his research career elsewhere. With W. E. Thrift's recommendation he secured it and, as a young experimental physicist in the 1920s, he knew there was one place above all others where he should go: the Cavendish Laboratory at Cambridge.

It has been remarked before that we might be forgiven today for supposing that Cambridge in those years was exclusively concerned with recruiting spies. It was not so. The Cavendish was the world's foremost physics laboratory. This it owed to the director, Lord Rutherford, perhaps the greatest of all experimental physicists, who gathered around him a brilliant team. When Walton arrived, three of the staff were Nobel prize winners and within weeks they were joined by a fourth; of his contemporaries in the next seven years, no less than six were so honoured. Admission to such company was no easy matter, but Walton succeeded thanks to a reference from the Trinity geology professor, John Joly, a scientist of international repute who knew Rutherford personally. It may also have helped that the Cavendish director, a New Zealander, had himself been an 1851 scholar in his day.

Walton arrived at the laboratory in October 1927. It was an inauspicious start. Through a misunderstanding of his own he was late for the start of term, and when he eventually got to Cambridge he could not at first find the Cavendish, which was in a narrow alley. None of the passers-by whom he asked had heard of the place. No harm was done, however, and he was soon down to work with that year's other newcomers, attending lectures by Rutherford and others and learning the practical ways of physics research in Cambridge.

Physics is a broad subject embracing many disciplines, but the focus of research at Rutherford's Cavendish was the nucleus of the atom. Rutherford himself had contributed more than any other scientist to the understanding of the nucleus which prevailed in 1927. The notion that all the matter in the world, be it solid, liquid or gas, is made up of minute particles dated back to ancient Greece. The word 'atom' was coined to describe the most minute of these minute particles, a unit so small that it could not be made smaller. Even when Rutherford began studying science it was still generally believed that these basic building blocks of matter were solid and indivisible, like billiard balls. It had, however, been discovered that atoms were not all the same. Oxygen atoms, for example, had been found to be about 16 times heavier than hydrogen atoms, which were known to be the lightest of all. A whole hierarchy had been established, with hydrogen having an approximate atomic weight of 1 and oxygen 16, while others fitted in elsewhere: lithium at 7, beryllium at 9, sodium at 23 and silicon at 28, to take some lighter elements. Though they might differ in weight, they were still billiard balls, until a series of discoveries at the turn of the century proved otherwise. On the one hand, heavy, 'radioactive' elements were found whose atoms 'spat out' smaller particles. And on the other hand, a new particle called an electron was identified, which was 1,840 times lighter than the hydrogen atom and which existed inside atoms. The billiard ball was dead; the atom was clearly a complex affair, with a good deal going on inside it.

Rutherford played an important part in these discoveries, but his inquiries had just begun. He set about analysing the particles emitted by one radioactive element, radium, and found that they could be divided into three types, which he called alpha, beta and gamma rays. The alpha rays he found most interesting. They were made up of relatively heavy particles, with an atomic weight of 4, the same as helium atoms. And for a short distance they travelled very fast. So he put them to use. Employing a relatively simple apparatus, he refined the rays until he had a fine beam of alpha particles, and then he directed this beam at a thin film of gold.

What happened was surprising. Most of the alpha particles passed straight through the film as if it was not there. This was to be expected, since it was generally believed by this time that atoms must be made up of clouds of lesser particles through which an alpha particle would pass unhindered. Occasionally, however, one of the alpha particles bounced back. How could this happen? In a remarkable piece of deduction Rutherford produced the answer: atoms *were* made up of clouds of tiny electrons, but at the heart of each atom lay a solid nucleus, off which the odd alpha particle would rebound. Refined by the great Niels Bohr, this theory offered a completely new understanding of the atom. It was a solar system with the nucleus as its sun, around which, in well-defined orbits, span the electrons.

Rutherford and Bohr had performed a work of genius, but answers usually beg more questions and this case was no exception. Scientists immediately wanted to know more about the nucleus. Observations, calculations and more experiments of the kind described above yielded much information. The nucleus, it was found, was usually a cluster of particles, each with an atomic weight of about 1. Some of these particles carried a positive charge, and some did not. The former were called protons. The orbiting electrons carried a negative charge which exactly balanced the positive charges of the protons inside the nucleus.

One more of Rutherford's early experiments is relevant. He put some radium in a container of nitrogen and found that there was an escape of protons. It seemed that the heavy alpha particles spat out by the radium were striking the nitrogen nuclei and chipping small fragments off them. This was another milestone, for it meant that the nucleus, the core of the atom, could be broken open. When we want to understand how something works, we take it apart. When scientists wanted to know how the nucleus worked, they had to do the same. With the alpha particles naturally expelled by radium, Rutherford had found a tool, albeit a primitive one, for doing just this.

This is where we return to Ernest Walton. It was December

1927, he was 24 and he had come to the end of his introductory term at the Cavendish. He now had to decide what research project to pursue, and the task he chose was to investigate ways of producing an artificial beam of particles which might prove a more flexible tool than natural alpha rays. It was already widely recognised that such a beam, which could be turned on and off and adjusted to strength, would be invaluable in breaking open the nucleus.

For the next year Walton struggled in vain with two different schemes for creating particle beams. Natural alpha particles, as they leave a radium atom, travel at speeds measured in thousands of miles per second, and to produce a comparable beam requires either enormous electrical voltages or considerable ingenuity. Walton employed the latter. First, he tried spinning electrons in a circular field in the hope that, as in a slingshot, they would accelerate sufficiently to form a useful beam. When that failed, he tried to accelerate particles by shooting them through a line of cylinders carrying high-frequency currents. The intention was that they should jump in speed with each cylinder they passed through, but again this 'linear' apparatus could not be persuaded to work. These failures did not mean that Walton's ideas were bad. On the contrary, both techniques have since been developed successfully. He was unlucky, but his time was not wasted.

Sharing his laboratory were two other men, T. E. Allibone and John Cockcroft, and above the racket of their machinery they struck up good working relationships which were in time to prove most fruitful. Allibone remembered the newcomer from Ireland as 'an extremely likeable man, full of humour and original ideas, exceptionally clever with his hands and quite capable of making spare parts for watches'.[7] Cockcroft, the most senior of the three, was a quiet man with a tendency to absent-mindedness. On occasion he would switch on his apparatus and then go out, leaving his colleagues to rescue his forgotten equipment before it overheated or fell apart. He was also obliging almost to a fault, always helping others, and indeed his engineering expertise proved useful to Walton more than once in those early days.

Despite his setbacks, Walton managed to impress Rutherford. This was vital, not least because the great man's support was needed if, as Walton now hoped, his scholarship was to be extended for a second year. Rutherford, who was both a referee and a member of the scholarship panel, settled the matter by pronouncing Walton to be 'an original and able man' who 'had tackled a very difficult problem with energy and skill'.[8] The stage was now set for the great Cockcroft-Walton experiment, which was inspired by a letter from a Russian theoretician, George Gamow, raising the possibility that there might be a tunnel into the nucleus.

Great forces are at work in the atom. They not only bind the particles of the nucleus together and maintain the electrons in their orbit; they also protect it from certain forms of attack. To dismantle the nucleus, to break it apart and examine its component parts, scientists had to reckon with these forces. Gamow had been thinking about this problem, and particularly the question of how the various particles spat out by radium were able to burst through the barrier that holds the nucleus together from the inside. Applying a new theoretical approach known as quantum mechanics, he showed that it was possible for particles to beat the barrier even if they did not carry sufficient energy to surmount it — as though they were passing through a tunnel. Then Gamow reflected that, if particles could get out of the nucleus at relatively low energies, they could also get in. In other words, the tunnel might work in both directions, and enormous electrical voltages might not be needed to attack the nucleus.

He sent his idea to the Cavendish, where Cockcroft became intrigued and did some calculations. He worked out that, if Gamow were right, 300,000 volts should be sufficient to penetrate the nucleus, a fraction of the power previously thought necessary. Cockcroft persuaded Rutherford to allow him to build an apparatus to test the theory. Rutherford decided it was a job for two and turned to Walton. 'I was slightly surprised, and slightly relieved, to be approached,' Walton recalled much later. 'I wasn't getting very far with my linear job, and here was a machine you could definitely build, although you didn't know whether you would get any results out of it.'

Three years passed before they knew the gamble was justified. The machine, vastly more complex than Walton's earlier projects, cost the Cavendish well over £1,500, a huge commitment for a laboratory constantly short of cash. The 'string and sealing wax' age of science was not far behind, and physicists were still building their apparatus from whatever bits and pieces they could lay hands on. Timber was used and re-used; metal tubes were improvised from bicycle frames; students learned glass-blowing so that they could make their own equipment. Cockcroft and Walton were aiming to link together a complicated array of different machines, demanding of each of them much more than it had done before. Dozens of individual parts were to be taken to the limit of their capabilities and dozens more would have to be designed and made anew — a task tailor-made for the deft and ingenious Walton.

The apparatus was to have five main components. First, a transformer to raise the voltage to 300,000 volts. Second, a device called a rectifier to convert this alternating current (AC) into a steady current. Third, a hydrogen gas container from which protons (hydrogen atoms without their electrons) could be drawn. Fourth, the accelerator tube in which these protons would be catapulted to high speeds by the voltage, and fifth, the 'target' and equipment to observe the results. Around this core was a further array of equipment feeding and monitoring the separate parts. The rectifiers and the accelerator tube (both made of glass cylinders) had to be pumped free of air, so special vacuum pumps were needed. The voltage applied to the protons in the accelerator tube had to be exactly right, so it had to be checked by measuring the sparks between two large aluminium spheres. Some parts of the apparatus needed their own power supply, so car batteries were attached here and there.

The transformer was ordered from the engineering firm Metropolitan-Vickers, where both Cockcroft and Allibone had once worked. It had to be exceptionally powerful yet small enough to fit in the laboratory, so a special machine was built incorporating a number of innovations. The rectifiers, which worked a little like valves, were at first copied from a type in the shape of a rugby ball then in use in X-ray machines. They were glass, and it was soon found that this shape could not withstand high voltages, so a new type was developed using thick glass cylinders. The same cylinders were used in the accelerator tube. The pumps, too, were novel, employing a special oil just developed by Metropolitan-Vickers. The same oil, called Apiezon, also proved invaluable as a component of the high-grade plasticine used to vacuum-seal the joints in the rectifiers and the accelerator tube. For every part of the new machine that worked, another failed. The two men went up numerous blind alleys, expending weeks of work on ideas that eventually had to be abandoned. They were fortunate, however, in being able to draw on the huge pool of expertise at the Cavendish — one of the reasons for the laboratory's pre-eminence was that researchers could count on first-class guidance in every field of nuclear physics.

After a year of work, Cockcroft and Walton were able to start testing the machine, a process every bit as laborious as building it. Their results, they knew, would be useless if their workmanship was in any way faulty. Impurities in the proton beam, leaks in the vacuums or poor calibration of the measuring instruments could simply not be tolerated. So rather than inserting a target and trying straight away to split atoms, they tinkered and tested for months. Then in June 1930 they began firing protons at certain elements, but their first results were unclear and the effort to clarify what was happening ended when the transformer failed. It was frustrating, but both men concluded that they were simply asking too much of their machinery. It could not perform reliably at the voltage levels they required; they needed to build something bigger. Their prayers were answered when, in the New Year, a larger room fell vacant and they were given permission and money to transfer their work and start on a new machine.

We know now that they had come very close to success in that summer of 1930; that even the smaller machine had the capacity to split the atomic nucleus. We also know that another team of scientists in California, led by Ernest Lawrence, might equally have done it that year. But they did not.

Given the frustrations of their work, it was fortunate that Cockcroft and Walton made a happy partnership. In some ways they were alike, both nonconformists with spartan habits, serious, even-tempered and dedicated. In other respects there was a contrast. Cockcroft was six years older, a war veteran and married. He had been at the Cavendish five years longer, had a lecturing post and a part-time job as assistant to a senior member of the Cavendish staff. He was also a respected figure in the university, much in demand for administrative tasks. His connections helped make him, in Walton's words, a 'good scrounger' for money and apparatus. His many commitments, however, took him away from the laboratory a good deal, leaving much of the practical work to his younger collaborator. In another partnership this might have caused tension, but Walton has said: 'I can't recall a single instance of the slightest thing you might call a minor row. I loved all the construction work and indeed I did most of it, so I had no grudge.'

To step up their power supply to the new target of 700,000 volts, Cockcroft now developed an ingenious circuit called a voltage multiplier, capable of doubling the voltage and then doubling it again. Other features were also re-designed, particularly the 'target' and observation section, which previously could only be used when lying on the floor. Now it became a box, like a tea-chest, with a seat inside. By the end of 1931 the new apparatus was ready for testing. Cavendish memoirs from this period almost always include a description of the two men perched atop ladders pressing plasticine into leaky vacuum seals. For three months they tinkered, experimented, measured and repaired. They were fascinated and delighted by their machine, absorbed in proving its power. At the same time, in California, Lawrence's team were enjoying the same experience with their new particle accelerator, the cyclotron. The high voltages were simply thrilling.

For one man, this was not enough. Walton recalls: 'Rutherford came in and asked what we were doing, and said something like this: "Nobody's interested in the measurements you are taking; get on with it and see if these particles will actually do anything."' The next morning Walton was, as so often, alone with the machine. He began warming it up in the usual way. He would turn it on, pumps would rumble and the transformer would hum. The rectifiers, a glass column now three metres tall, would glow as the voltage climbed. Protons, leaving the hydrogen gas container, entered the top of the accelerator tube where the voltage whipped them into a fast-moving beam, and then, with a bang or a flash, something would fail. A repair was made, and the process began again until, after a couple of hours, the power reached 600,000 volts and the beam of particles was moving, safely and steadily, at the required speed. Walton, ducking low, now crossed to the hut at the foot of the accelerator tube, sat inside and peered into a microscope. As the beam struck a target of the element lithium, he watched a card, covered with crystals, next to the target. This arrangement had been set up in accordance with Rutherford's demand to 'see if these particles will actually do anything'. As Walton watched, there were tiny flashes on the card. He climbed out, reduced the voltage and looked again. Fewer flashes. He turned the proton beam off. No flashes at all.

Walton called Cockcroft, who rushed over to see the flashes. He brought in Rutherford, who was squeezed into the hut to see them too. All three knew what the flashes meant: protons, with a weight of 1, were entering lithium nuclei, which have a weight of 7, and creating new units with a weight of 8. These were then splitting into two parts, each with a weight of 4— helium nuclei. They must be helium nuclei, the scientists knew, because only helium nuclei, bursting out of the target, would make those flashes when they struck the crystals on the card. The nucleus, in other words, had been split; helium had been manufactured from lithium and hydrogen and a scientific tool had been created which could vastly extend man's understanding of the structure of matter. The closest that Walton would come in later years to admitting he was by now excited was to say it was 'very pleasant to discover you hadn't wasted your time'. Certainly there were no immediate celebrations, for Rutherford set the two men to work verifying their results. Winifred Walton, however, has recalled that her husband, then her fiance, wrote to her that night, 'greatly excited', describing what had happened. 'I was probably the first person in the world to hear about it,' she said.[9]

A few days later the two scientists wrote to *Nature*. The press interest in the announcement took Walton by surprise. Long and sometimes muddled articles appeared in the papers, along with photographs, cartoons and editorials. Impressed, perhaps, by the play *Wings over Europe*, the leader writers tended to ask for the atom to be treated with respect. 'Let it be split, so long as it does not explode,' said the *Daily Mirror*.[10]

Explode, as we know, it did. In 1945, with the detonation of two atomic bombs over Japan, the political world was transformed. The inner workings of the nucleus, it had been found, could provide explosives of enormous power and, into the bargain, a new means of generating electricity. The nuclear bomb was regarded as mere science fiction in the Cavendish of 1932, but nuclear energy was the subject of lively discussion. For the Cockcroft-Walton experiments had shown that when the nucleus split there was a considerable release of energy. Indeed, they had provided the first practical proof of Einstein's celebrated equation relating mass and energy, $E=mc^2$. Cockcroft told a newspaper interviewer that, with the success of the accelerator, scientists were now 'on the right path'[11] towards tapping this energy, while Rutherford maintained that any attempt to do so would be wasteful and fruitless. Both were wrong, for it was by a quite different route, the intensive study of the radioactive elements, that physicists came to discover the nuclear chain reaction that makes possible both the bombs and the power stations.

The accelerator opened the way for a quest that was less fateful, but which proved of equal grandeur. Atom-smashing is today a science in its own right, occupying thousands of researchers in hundreds of laboratories around the world. Machines resembling underground race-tracks, kilometres in circumference, hurl particles at each other at energies measured in hundreds of billions of volts. These gigantic descendants of the machine built by Cockcroft and Walton have brought man tantalisingly close to a new understanding of matter which may shed light at once on the heart of the atom and on the origin of the Universe.

It is in some ways an anticlimax to have to say that in 1934 Ernest Walton simply stepped aside from all this. For two years, he and Cockcroft remained at the cutting edge of research, publishing important papers and engaging in scientific controversy. In October 1933 they were invited to the Solvay conference in Brussels, a gathering of many of the outstanding physicists of the day, including not only Rutherford, Bohr, Lawrence and Gamow but also Enrico Fermi, Werner Heisenberg, Pierce Langevin and Marie Curie. Within a year, however, Walton was back in Trinity College, Dublin, his research career effectively over at the age of 31, settling into the quiet, industrious life he was to pursue until the day, 40 years later, when he retired.

He was even, during the Second World War, to pass up a pressing invitation to return to the scientific mainstream. In a letter specially delivered to him through the British embassy in Dublin, probably in 1944, Walton was invited to join a British team going to America to take part in an important, but unidentified, military research project. The letter was written by James Chadwick, a distinguished former member of the Cavendish staff. Walton consulted the Provost, who declared that the physics department and the university were already running on a minimum of staff because so many men had left to join the British forces, and he could not be spared. Walton accepted this verdict without demur. The research project he thus declined a share in — although he could not have known it — was the development of the atomic bomb.

Walton's life changed course dramatically in 1934, but given the circumstances of the time and of the man the new direction was not altogether surprising. Trinity offered him not only a teaching post, but also the extremely rare honour of a fellowship of the university granted purely on the basis of his 'distinguished merit' (candidate fellows were normally required to sit an examination). He was still fond of his old college and he knew that the physics department had been reformed, with an infusion of new blood. At the Cavendish, many of his contemporaries were making similar moves and the great team of researchers was breaking up. This was, moreover, during the Depression and jobs were scarce; after years existing on short-term scholarships, Walton was naturally eager to start salaried employment, particularly because it would allow him to marry the girl he had known since school and with whom he had corresponded through the Cavendish days: Winifred Wilson.

That he should voluntarily have relinquished the forefront of research when he reached Dublin was a reflection of personal taste. Excitement was not something he valued and his experience of public attention, particularly press attention, left him sceptical about the glamour of scientific success. Practical factors were also at work. Trinity had little money to spend on apparatus, and Walton's field was perhaps the most expensive of all. Over several years, he did construct an accelerator, but it was never to yield results of importance.

He had been hired to teach and he applied himself to doing that well. The deft fingers and ingenuity of mind were again invaluable; generations of graduates testify in particular to his talent for simultaneously explaining and performing a complicated experiment in front of a lecture theatre full of students. Walton became acting head of physics during the Second World War and full professor in 1946, and under his long stewardship the department grew steadily in numbers and resources — the stagnation of earlier years was forgotten. He served for many years on the governing board of the university and, as one of Ireland's few really distinguished scientists, was in constant demand to sit on government and other committees. In the course of these years, he and his wife settled in the comfortable Dublin district of Dartry and brought up two sons and two daughters, all of whom were to choose careers in science.

Ernest Walton took one more bow upon the stage of international physics. In 1951 he and John Cockcroft, who had by then been knighted and was head of the British Atomic Energy Research Establishment, were awarded the Nobel prize for physics. It was fully 19 years since they had first seen those tiny flashes which told them they had split the nucleus, but such a delay is not unique in Nobel history. The academy made it clear that the award recognised not only a fundamental advance in science but a step which, as the intervening years had shown, provided the stimulus for many other such advances. The work of Walton and Cockcroft, said the Nobel citation read out at the traditional ceremony in Stockholm, 'may be said to have produced a totally new epoch in nuclear research.'[12]

CLAUDE AUCHINLECK

1884–1981

Military Leader

Thomas G. Fraser

CLAUDE AUCHINLECK

Ulster's involvement in the fortunes of British India began on 22 June 1781 when Lord Macartney landed at Madras to assume the office of President of Fort St George; it ended on 1 December 1947 when the Supreme Commander of the armed forces of the new Dominions of India and Pakistan, Field-Marshal Sir Claude Auchinleck, took off for the last time from Delhi's Palam airport. Auchinleck's departure marked the end of a connection which had brought Ulstermen to the forefront of the Raj: Henry and John Lawrence who had laid the basis of British power in the Punjab, the former to die defending the Residency at Lucknow during the great upheaval of 1857, the latter to become Viceroy; the ferocious John Nicholson who fell at the Kashmir Gate leading the British assault on Delhi in 1857; Clandeboye's Marquess of Dufferin and Ava whose period as Viceroy in the 1880s coincided with the springing to life of an Indian political awareness which in time brought British rule to an end. That Auchinleck presided over the armed forces of India throughout the critical period of independence and partition would in itself justify a study of his distinguished career but his historical importance rests even more upon his contribution to the allied victory in the Second World War. For over a year, from June 1941 to August 1942, it fell to him as Supreme Commander in the Middle East to direct the one active British battlefront against the seemingly irresistible power of Hitler's Germany. His prolonged duel with Rommel's *Afrika Korps,* ending in his victory at the First Battle of Alamein and almost immediate dismissal by Winston Churchill, has become one of the most controversial series of events in the history of the war.

Claude John Eyre Auchinleck's ancestry combined two distinctive Irish traditions. His mother, Mary Eleanor Eyre, came of a long-established, if rather impoverished, Galway family. His father, Colonel John Auchinleck of the Royal Horse Artillery, was an Ulster-Scot whose family was recorded in the Middle Ages as living in the parish of Auchinleck in the hills of south Ayrshire. The precise date when the family joined in the movement of Lowland Scots to Ulster is not known but in the late seventeenth century the Rev. James Auchinleck was rector of Cleenish in County Fermanagh. For the next two hundred years the Auchinlecks lived in Fermanagh and Tyrone, marrying amongst the gentry of those counties and finding a living either on the land or as clergymen of the Church of Ireland. Like so many from such a background, John Auchinleck broke from that tradition by entering the military service of the Crown. His eldest son, Claude, was born in 1884 but when still a small child went out to India where Colonel Auchinleck was commanding the artillery at Bangalore.[1] Thus began an attachment to the subcontinent which was to become the abiding passion of his life, ending only amid the tragedies of 1947. Two things stand out from Auchinleck's background and early life: his sense of identity as an Ulsterman and his commitment to India.

To understand Claude Auchinleck it is necessary to know something of the Indian army which he joined as a Second Lieutenant in 1903. It was the descendant of the armies of the East India Company, separate in almost every respect from its British counterpart with which its relations were not always easy. India held no attraction for those members of the aristocracy and landed gentry who formed the officer corps of the pre-1914 British army, for its dusty cantonments were too remote from the centres of influence and social entertainment in Whitehall and St James's. Winston Churchill, who served there with a British regiment, devoted most of his energies to intriguing a way out of a country which he recognised as the cornerstone of Britain's world power but which he intensely disliked.[2] But to young men like Auchinleck, possessed of neither money nor influence, it offered an interesting, and at times exciting, career. The men they commanded came overwhelmingly from the so-called 'martial races' of north-west India, their favoured status being the result of the support they had given to the British during the great Mutiny of 1857. They were volunteers who enlisted because military service was closely associated with the most prized possession of the Indian peasant, land. Recruitment was a family affair, each volunteer having to prove that his father owned a plot of land, however small, and be vouched for by relations or friends from his village. Such men fought and died, not for the British Empire, but for the honour of a regiment which had become part of their extended family. Led by men like Auchinleck, who knew their customs and families, they could be ranked amongst the finest soldiers in the world. It was in such a unit, the 62nd Punjabis, formed from Sikhs, Muslims and Rajputs, that Auchinleck learned the essential skills of a regimental officer in the decade before the outbreak of war in 1914.

With the British army fully stretched in France and Flanders, it fell to the Indian army to sustain the major part of the war with Turkey. It was a cruel test for the Muslims under Auchinleck's command, for they were being asked to fight against their spiritual head, the Sultan of Turkey who was also Caliph of Islam. Although he knew it was a risk to ask Muslims to fire on their co-religionists, and some men at first hesitated to do so, the trust which had been built up in peactime prevailed and any problems were transient. The 62nd Punjabis had, in fact, been on their way to France when the Turks entered the war but were retained in Egypt for the defence of the Suez Canal. It was there, in February 1915, that Auchinleck had his first experience of war when his battalion helped repulse the Turkish army's attempt to cross the Canal. Most of his war service, however, was in that most ill-starred of campaigns, Mesopotamia, in fights that he later recalled as hard and desperate, conducted in terrible conditions. Ill-conceived and badly executed, the Mesopotamian campaign saw the encirclement of General Charles Townshend and his command at Kut-al-Amara on the Tigris in the spring of 1916. Ferocious fighting, in which

Auchinleck took a full part, failed to prevent the humiliating surrender of Townshend's force. It was a blow which seriously damaged British prestige in the East but it proved to be the prelude to a complete reorganisation of the campaign. By early 1917 the Imperial forces were on the offensive and Auchinleck had that prized possession of every officer, command of his regiment in battle. When the war ended in November 1917, he was Brigade-Major to the 52nd Brigade, clearly identified as one of the 'coming men' of the Indian army. Fortunate, of course, to have survived these years of heavy fighting, he had experience both of field command and staff work.[3] Even more fortunate seemed to be his marriage, in 1920, to a vivacious young Scots girl who had been brought up in the United States, Jessie Stewart. Fifteen years his junior, she brought a fresh dimension to the life of a man who had hitherto known little more than the masculine world of regimental life and who was always inclined to be solitary and introspective.

When the Second World War broke out Auchinleck was ideally placed for senior command. He had both studied and taught at the Staff College at Quetta, and commanded his battalion and then the Peshawar Brigade. By 1936 he was a Major-General and Deputy Chief of the General Staff, having earned a high reputation as a mountain fighter in command of operations on the North-West Frontier in 1933 and 1935. With the growing threat of war in Asia and Europe, not to mention India's own rapid constitutional advance towards self-government, the questions of the country's defensive needs and its ability to contribute to an Imperial war effort needed urgent professional attention. As Chairman of the Indian army's Modernization Committee in 1938 and then a member of Lord Chatfield's Committee on Indian defence, he was largely responsible for drawing up the basic guidelines needed to reverse years of neglect when the army had been little more than an internal police force. When the Polish crisis grew in the summer of 1939 the Auchinlecks were on leave in the United States and at home. Ordered to return to India to prepare the 3rd Indian Division at Meerut, Auchinleck was on board his ship at Greenock on 3 September when he heard Neville Chamberlain's broadcast that the country was at war with Germany.[4]

As the war settled into its first uneasy winter, it was inevitable that an officer of Auchinleck's stamp would not long be left in Meerut. Most of the promising officers in the British service, John Dill, Alan Brooke, Harold Alexander and Bernard Montgomery amongst them, were commanding corps, divisions or brigades with Lord Gort's British Expeditionary Force in France. It was, then, hardly surprising that early in 1940 he was brought home to organise and command the new IV Corps which was scheduled to join Gort's command in the Lille sector. Even so, it is important to realise what a new experience it was for him to command British troops in England, for he did not 'belong' to the British army; nor, for that matter, did he think of himself as an Englishman. But Auchinleck and his Corps never saw service in France: on 9 April Adolf Hitler, in one of those bold and imaginative strokes which had marked his career since the occupation of the Rhineland, attacked Denmark and Norway, leaving the British government grasping for any expedient which might retrieve the situation. Desperate attempts to halt the Germans in southern and central Norway failed; all that remained was to attempt the recapture of the crucial northern port of Narvik, whose importance for the nearby Swedish iron ore fields had been a prime reason for Hitler's move. On 28 April Auchinleck was appointed commander of the military forces in northern Norway, under the overall command of Admiral Lord Cork. It was then the only active front against the Germans and Auchinleck had every expectation that the necessary men and resources would be forthcoming. However, on 10 May, as he was sailing north, the whole character of the war was transformed with the beginning of the *blitzkrieg* in the west. Narvik had become an irrelevance for the new government under Winston Churchill which had to devote all its energies and resources to the Battle of France. On 24 May it decided to evacuate Norway but not before the port of Narvik had been destroyed. It had become a forlorn campaign in which Auchinleck's makeshift force of British, French, Norwegians and Poles had to fight tough German mountain troops backed with almost total air superiority; and this in the secret, but heartbreaking, knowledge that Norway was not to be held. Nevertheless, orders were carried out. Narvik was taken and its facilities destroyed and then on 7 June, having overseen the evacuation of his troops, Auchinleck sailed from the port of Harstad.[5]

In its own way the Norwegian campaign had exposed the allies' failure to prepare for the kind of war which Hitler had unleashed upon them but it was as nothing compared with the debacle which unfolded in France. Ten days after Auchinleck's return, the French signed an armistice with Hitler at the clearing in the forest of Compiegne which had witnessed their triumph in 1918. By then Gort's army had been evacuated from Dunkirk, albeit at the cost of all their heavy equipment. Less widely known, but significant for Auchinleck's future, was the fate of the 51st Highland Division which, swept along with the wreckage of the French Tenth Army, was surrounded and forced to surrender, though not outfought, at St Valery-en-Caux by the 7th Panzer Division commanded by Major-General Erwin Rommel. What stood between Hitler and total victory were the continuing ability of the Royal Navy to deny him passage of the Channel and the skills of Fighter Command. Had the *Wehrmacht* landed on the south coast it would have been met by an army which still had plenty of spirit but precious little else. It was the measure of Auchlinleck's rising reputation that he was given command of the 5th Corps on the south coast. He did not stay there long. On the weekend of 12 July he was at Chequers as guest of the Prime Minister who clearly formed a high impression of him for, a week later, as part of a major reorganisation of senior commanders, he was promoted G.O.C.-in-C. Southern Command. In short he was the man immediately responsible for repulsing a German invasion of southern England.[6] 'Yet', as his friend and biographer, John Connell, wrote of this period, 'he was not English: he was a

Northern Irishman of Scots extraction'.[7] In the event of an invasion his strategy was to hold the Germans on the beaches before they could consolidate and bring across their heavy equipment. His work in Southern Command over the summer and autumn of 1940 provoked a series of bitter clashes with his immediate subordinate and successor in 5th Corps, Bernard Montgomery, a matter of crucial significance for the subsequent reputations of both men. Of more immediate importance, the organisation of Southern Command brought him increasingly to the attention of the Prime Minister, reinforcing Churchill's favourable view of his potential.

His next promotion was the obvious one. In November 1940 he was appointed Commander-in-Chief in India with the rank of full General. He did not hold the appointment long, for in the spring of 1941 he was largely responsible for an initiative which convinced the Prime Minister and his superiors in London that he was capable of the vigorous action vital to a successful prosecution of the war. Pro-Axis forces in Iraq had established contact with the Germans, threatening to overturn the British position in the country, with disastrous consequences for oil supplies. It was Auchinleck's prompt diversion of Indian troops to Basra which was instrumental in securing the situation. His action seemed so much more positive than that of the Commander-in-Chief Middle East, Archibald Wavell, who was preoccupied with the situation in Egypt and the eastern Mediterranean. Here, Churchill was convinced, was the fresh mind the war effort needed.[8]

Wavell had been responsible for the first British victories of the war. With minimal resources he had humiliated the Italian armies in North Africa, prompting Hitler to intervene, and he had conquered the Italian empire in east Africa. But Churchill had never warmed to him, blaming him, quite unfairly, for Britain's failure to give adequate support to Greece and Crete. When Wavell's final Western Desert offensive failed in May 1941, Churchill decided he had to go. On 21 June Auchinleck was informed that he and Wavell were to exchange posts. He had, so Churchill confided in President Roosevelt, the energy necessary to reinvigorate the Middle East theatre.[9] Auchinleck now assumed command of the British Empire's principal land front against the Axis, with a wide variety of military and political problems stretching from Northern Iraq to the Western Desert. No part of this vast area could be ignored, not least because the day after Auchinleck's appointment Hitler's invasion of the Soviet Union raised the awesome spectre of victorious German armies on his northern flank. Throughout his entire period of command he had to be prepared to meet that threat.

Nevertheless, the Western Desert had primacy. When Hitler decided in February 1941 that his Italian allies needed support in North Africa, his choice as commander was Erwin Rommel. Rommel was destined to become one of the war's legends, as much to his opponents as to his own men. To the British he became the 'Desert Fox'. To the German public he became the 'Soldier in the Sun', whose exploits, carefully fostered by the Propaganda Ministry, served as an exotic distraction from the grinding struggle on the Russian Front. He was a fine tactician with invaluable experience from Poland and France on how to direct armoured warfare. He was a brilliant improviser, an essential virtue given the tenuous nature of his supply lines and the relative indifference of a High Command obsessed with the war in the East. Above all, he had the 'killer instinct', and was equally ruthless with his enemy and with his own troops, whom he was prepared to drive far beyond what might normally be expected of them. By the summer of 1941 the German *Afrika Korps* under his command comprised two Panzer Divisions, the 15th and the 21st, and the 90th Light Division; he had, in addition, six Italian divisions. His German troops had all the confidence of men who knew that they were winning the war.[10]

In contrast, Auchinleck's Middle East command was a polyglot affair of British, Indian, Australian, New Zealand and South African forces with very mixed traditions and training. South Africa's participation in the war was a matter of acute domestic controversy, while the Australian and New Zealand governments were increasingly uneasy that their best troops were in the Middle East at a time when Japanese intentions were so worrying. Nevertheless, Auchinleck's principal problem in confronting the *Afrika Korps* lay in British inexperience in armoured warfare. Although Britain had pioneered the tank in the First World War, senior commanders had presided over its virtual demise during the 1920s and 1930s. This was the product of a social and military conservatism which was to cost Britain dear in the early years of the Second World War. Not only were the cavalrymen who commanded the British armour markedly inferior to their German counterparts but Britain had yet to produce a tank capable of matching the Panzer Mark III and IV of the *Afrika Korps*. No tank in Auchinleck's command fired anything heavier than a two-pound shell; Rommel had tanks firing 14-pound shells and nothing less than 4-pounders. There was no proper anti-tank gun, while the German 88mm gun killed tanks with deadly efficiency.[11] Supplies and reinforcements had to come by a 12,000 mile sea journey during which tanks and other vehicles deteriorated so badly that weeks of work were required to make them battle-worthy.[12] Yet Auchinleck had one clear advantage over Rommel — the regular flow of high-grade Ultra intelligence derived from the decoders at Bletchley Park. In fact, this intelligence proved to be a somewhat mixed blessing. The desert battles were too fast moving for the signals to be consistently useful in assessing Rommel's intentions. But they enabled Churchill to read Rommel's constant complaints of lack of supplies. His pressure on Auchinleck to mount prompt offensive action to take advantage of the perceived weakness of the *Afrika Korps* underestimated Rommel's talent for improvisation and his willingness to push his troops beyond normal limits: but it did fuel the Prime Minister's growing frustration and ultimate discontent.[13]

Auchinleck's priority was the creation of his main striking force, the Eighth Army. For its commander he chose General Sir Alan Cunningham, who had made his reputation in the conquest of East Africa. Once the new Eighth Army's men and equipment had been made desert-worthy, Auchinleck planned a major offensive to relieve the isolated garrison of Tobruk and drive the Axis army from Libya, but he was not prepared to do so until this process had been completed. This inevitably brought him into conflict with the Prime Minister, who was anxious for an early offensive and felt compelled to offer advice, encouragement, exhortation and downright interference in operational matters which were properly the responsibility of the Commander-in-Chief. As early as August he was depressed by the news from Auchinleck that action could not be expected before November.[14]

The Eighth Army's carefully-prepared offensive, Operation 'Crusader', began on 18 November 1941. It started well, taking Rommel by surprise, but the German army's powers of recupe-ration were formidable. Rommel's riposte with his two Panzer divisions so decimated Cunningham's inferior tanks that by the 23rd Cunningham was ready to abandon the operation. On the following day Rommel gathered together his armour and directed a massive raid on Cunningham's rear with the object of breaking up the Eighth Army and advancing into Egypt. Months of planning and training had seemingly gone for nothing. Auchin-leck's response to this situation was cool and decisive. Undaunted by Rommel's boldness, he flew to Cunningham's headquarters on the 24th and issued clear instructions that the offensive was to be pursued. His confidence was backed by Ultra intelligence that the German armour was thinly stretched and its fuel resources low. But Cunningham had clearly lost the initiative to Rommel and on the 25th Auchlinleck decided to dismiss him. In his place he appointed General Neil Ritchie, one of Auchinleck's principal staff officers, who could execute his chief's intentions for an offensive he was determined to continue.[15]

Faced with the realisation that the British had not panicked, Rommel saw no alternative but to retreat. Had the British tanks and guns been equal to the task, his retreat might well have ended in rout but the Panzers' superior firepower saw them safely back to base. Auchinleck now moved to Eighth Army headquarters to direct the battle in person. His troops were still fighting hard. So were Rommel's, though he knew that his German soldiers were exhausted and that the Italian formations were fast disintegrating. The Axis retreat began on the night of 7-8 December and continued into the New Year. Tobruk was at last relieved and Rommel's army was relentlessly pushed back through Cyrenaica. On 2 January 1942 Auchinleck's forces took the key German supply base at Bardia. Further successes followed at Sollum and Halfaya where South African and Free French forces took 4,000 German and 10,000 Italian prisoners. By 11 January Rommel had been forced to retreat to his strong defensive position of El Agheila on the Gulf of Sirte. Auchinleck had won the first British land victory against the Germans of the Second World War. His army had lost 18,000 men to Rommel's 21,000 and the Axis forces had been pushed back almost 300 miles. The Italians, in particular, were bitterly resentful of Rommel's ruthless determination to save his German troops at their expense. The measure of Auchinleck's success was Hitler's order, on 5 December, that an entire *Flieger Korps* be transferred from his hard-pressed Russian front to the central Mediterranean and North Africa. Success had been achieved despite inferior and inadequate equipment, to the great benefit of the Eighth Army's self-confidence.[16] In January 1942 Auchinleck looked forward to the organisation of his supply lines, the re-supply and reinforcement of his army and the final offensive against the Axis forces.

But he had not destroyed Rommel's army in 'Crusader' and on a world scale Hitler and his allies still held the initiative. Moreover, on 7 December 1941 the Japanese attacked the American Pacific Fleet at Pearl Harbor, provoking a global conflict and threatening the destruction of the British Empire in Asia. On 15 February 1942 the great base of Singapore fell and four days later the first Japanese bombs fell on Australia. In the long term, American entry into the war guaranteed Allied victory but for the time being Axis forces seemed everywhere triumphant from Leningrad and Sevastopol to Rangoon and the Java Sea. As a result the reinforcements expected by Auchinleck were not forthcoming. The 18th Division which was *en route* to the Middle East was diverted to Malaya, where it was captured; the 17th Indian Division was held in India; and large numbers of Australian troops, and key New Zealand officers, were withdrawn from the Middle East for home defence. In such circumstances Rommel had no reason to feel unduly cast down by his reverse in Cyrenaica. As early as 5 January 1942 a supply convoy of nine ships with 55 tanks, 20 armoured cars and a number of anti-tank guns succeeded in reaching Tripoli. In the finely-drawn battle lines of North Africa it was, as one of Rommel's generals put it, 'as good as a victory in battle' and it set the resilient German commander immediately thinking of a renewed offensive. The crucial race for supplies now turned to Rommel's advantage just as the Japanese offensive was robbing Auchinleck. Hitler's prompt action meant that the *Luftwaffe* dominated the central Mediterranean at a time when the Royal Navy was at its weakest. In November 1941 the aircraft carrier *Ark Royal* and the battleship *Barham* were sunk by U boats: a month later Italian 'human torpedoes' cripplied the *Queen Elizabeth* and *Valiant* in Alexandria, while reinforcements were impossible with the loss of the Prince of *Wales* and *Repulse* off Malaya. The cumulative effect of all of this was to render transient the victory which Auchinleck and the Eighth Army had won so dearly. On 21 January, reinforced by convoys which had come across the Mediterranean, including an entire Italian division, Rommel counter-attacked, regaining a large area of Cyrenaica. Thereafter, for some three months, he and Auchinleck concentrated on rebuilding their strength for a final, decisive battle.

In the spring of 1942 the *Luftwaffe* controlled the central Mediterranean, ensuring a temporary Axis advantage in logistics. Determined not to forfeit this, and uneasily aware of the potential of the new American tanks which were reaching the Eighth Army, Rommel began his greatest desert offensive on 26 May. In the worst fighting the Middle East had yet seen, the Eighth Army was decisively beaten; its generals had still to master armoured warfare and its commander, Neil Ritchie, was no match for Rommel.

Auchinleck has been severely criticised both for his choice of Ritchie and for not taking direct control of the battle once it had become clear, as it was by 13 June, that the Eighth Army had been defeated.[17] His reluctance to do so stemmed from the wide-ranging nature of his command and his fear of what might happen to the Middle East should the Germans break the front in southern Russia. But it was a mistake, for on crucial occasions Ritchie ignored his directives with disastrous results, most obviously so in the case of Tobruk. The port, which had withstood an eight-month siege the previous year, had entered British mythology but Auchinleck, while determined to hold it if he could, had no desire to see a major portion of the Eighth Army invested in it. But Churchill still saw it through the prism of the previous year and Ritchie, despite Auchinleck's instructions to the contrary, began belated and inadequate measures to prepare Tobruk for a siege. Auchinleck should have ignored the pressure from the former and asserted his authority over the latter but did not do so; instead, 33,000 troops under the South African General Klopper fell back into the Tobruk perimeter and on 21 June, after a battle lasting less than a day, surrendered. It was, as Rommel later recorded, the 'high point' of the desert war; the following day he was promoted Field-Marshal.[18]

Coming as it did so soon after the debacle of Singapore, the fall of Tobruk seemed a cruel confirmation of the inadequacy of the British war effort. It came at a particularly embarrassing time for Churchill, who had flown to Washington for talks with Roosevelt and the American command and who now felt not just defeated but disgraced before his allies.[19] On his return he had to face a parliamentary motion of no confidence. This was an ominous situation for Auchinleck; so was the domestic situation of the South African leader, Field-Marshal Smuts. He had no time to ponder, for Rommel, now reinforced by the supplies he had taken at Tobruk, began what he intended to be the final destruction of the depleted Eighth Army and the capture of the great naval base of Alexandria and the Suez Canal. Had Auchinleck and his troops been broken, the consequences for the entire Allied war effort would have been disastrous. On 25 June, as the units of the Eighth Army retreated across the Egyptian frontier, Auchinleck dismissed Ritchie and assumed personal direction of the battle. Three days later Mussolini arrived in Africa to prepare for a triumphal entry into Cairo.

On the 24th Auchinleck had acknowledged to Churchill that his position was back to where it had been in 1941, except that the enemy now held Tobruk. Nonetheless, he planned to hold the enemy as far to the west as possible until the promised reinforcements enabled him to resume the offensive.[20] Auchinleck already knew where he would defend Egypt: not on the frontier, but only 100 miles from Alexandria at El Alamein where the sea protected his right flank and the Qattara Depression fifty miles inland his left. He had long been aware of its defensive potential and had prepared positions which every available soldier now hastened to reinforce. On 1 July Rommel began the Battle of Alamein and soon acknowledged the coolness and skill with which Auchinleck was countering his moves. Far from conducting a triumphal entry into Alexandria after a beaten enemy, for three days Rommel was outfought on the Alamein positions. Auchinleck's tactics were brutally simple: to strike wherever possible at the Italian formations, forcing the three German divisions to wear themselves out in a series of rescue missions which robbed the *Afrika Korps* of any initiative. It worked. On 3 July, to Rommel's dismay, the Ariete Armoured Division broke and ran, leading to the collapse of the Germans' main attack.[21] On the 9th a similar fate befell the Sabratha Division and two days later the bulk of the Trieste Division was destroyed. In an attempt to take the pressure off his Italian units, Rommel pressed a series of attacks by his German tanks but Auchinleck was not to be deflected from what had become a winning tactic. On the 15th most of the Brescia and Pavia Divisions were taken prisoner; two days later Rommel confessed to his wife that the British were systematically destroying his Italian formations and that his German units were too weak to sustain the fight alone.[22] After two months of fighting both sides were exhausted but the Germans succeeded in flying in men of the 164th Infantry Division from Crete. Between 21 and 27 July Auchinleck counter-attacked Rommel's positions but could not force a breakthrough. Substantial reinforcements of men and tanks were on their way; Auchinleck and his staff began to prepare plans to drive Rommel from Egypt and out of Africa. Back in Rome, a disconsolate Mussolini acknowledged a 'turning point' in his affairs.

Rommel's judgement on these battles was also clear; namely, that in halting the German offensive Auchinleck had done what mattered. The view in London was rather different. Deeply embarrassed by Tobruk, which had come after a series of disasters, Churchill desperately needed a victory. He had been unhappy with Auchinleck for some time and his view of affairs in the Middle East had not been helped by reports which seemed to suggest that further withdrawals had been contemplated. It was true that after Tobruk the fleet had left Alexandria for Haifa and that zealous officers in Cairo had begun the systematic burning of papers, in contrast to Auchinleck's cool handling of the Alamein front. Churchill now determined to see the situation for himself, together with Smuts, Wavell and the Chief of the General Staff, Alan Brooke. He arrived in Egypt on 3 August. Everyone, Auchinleck included, knew that the Eighth Army needed its own commander again but what seems to have convinced the Prime Minister that a complete change was necessary was Auchinleck's insistence that he could not go over to the offensive before late September. On 8 August Churchill's secretary arrived at Eighth Army headquarters with a personal letter for Auchinleck. It informed him that General Alexander was to take over as Commander-in-Chief Middle East, and that Montgomery would assume command of the Eighth Army. Auchinleck was offered a new command in Persia and Iraq, which he rightly saw as a consolation prize and refused. Churchill and his advisers may well have been right in thinking that the Middle East theatre needed new blood but Auchinleck's dismissal was brusque, to say the least. More insidious were subsequent allegations by Montgomery that he had taken over a defeated and defeatist command which he had ultimately galvanised into action. But such controversies lay in the future; for the time being Auchinleck was out of the war.[23]

It was not easy to see how he might return to high command. Doubts about his field ability were now entertained by both Brooke and Churchill, the latter having his prejudices powerfully reinforced by Montgomery's acid comments during a visit to Tunisia in February 1943; and Wavell still had the India command. Nevertheless, by May 1943 Churchill wished to relieve Wavell and replace him by Auchinleck, who seemed the ideal choice to lead an Indian army undergoing unprecedented expansion for the war against Japan. The solution was to appoint Wavell to the Indian Viceroyalty in succession to Lord Linlithgow, with Auchinleck as his Commander-in-Chief but with no operational responsibilities outside India, which were to come instead under a new South-East Asia Command. Auchinleck accepted, though with some reservations about his ability to work with Wavell and resentment that he was to have no control over operations in the field.[24] In fact, the next two years showed a harmonious trinity of Wavell, Auchinleck and the new head of South-East Asia Command, Lord Mountbatten. Under Auchinleck's command the Indian army expanded to two million, the largest volunteer army in history. He was now the Jang-i-Bat Sahib, the Lord of War, who knew from forty years' experience the hopes, concerns and potential of the Indian soldier. That knowledge pointed to the future, for he knew that the 'old' army based on certain castes and classes was no longer adequate for a force which was training to beat the Japanese and which would soon be at the service of an independent India. As a result, military service was encouraged on a national basis. Out of his command came the men of the 14th Army, an overwhelmingly Indian formation which defeated the Japanese in Burma and was the main 'British' front of the Asian war.

By the end of the war Auchinleck might well have felt that,

despite all the buffetings of previous years, he had reached a solid plateau of achievement. Promoted Field-Marshal in May 1946, he was widely respected in India for his sympathetic understanding of the country's transition to independence. Nevertheless, it proved to be a tragic time for him. Always a sensitive man, the denigration of his achievements at Alamein rankled. His marriage had collapsed during the war and ended in divorce, increasing his sense of isolation. On the day his baton was announced, a lady friend found him alone in his garden with no celebration planned.[25] One great passion remained, the Indian army and that, too, was under threat, for in March 1940 the Muslim League led by Muhammad Ali Jinnah had demanded the partition of India on religious grounds. By 1945 Jinnah commanded the allegiance of a majority of Indian Muslims and the British government could not proceed to Indian independence without accommodating his claim for Pakistan. In common with most of the British in India, Auchinleck found the concept of a separate Muslim state unconvincing, the more so in his case as partition clearly meant division of the armed forces, an outcome he could barely contemplate. In May 1946 he wrote a devastating critique of the military implications of 'Pakistan', concluding that the interests of the British Commonwealth could only be served by a united India.[26]

But Auchinleck, like Mahatma Gandhi, Jawaharlal Nehru and the leaders of the Indian National Congress, could not contain the 'Pakistan Demand' or the religious passions associated with it. In August 1946 the 'Great Calcutta Killing' ushered in a period of communal strife that spread throughout northern India in the winter of 1946-47. Faced with disintegration, in February 1947 the British government announced that Wavell would be replaced by Mountbatten whose task was to bring about a speedy resolution of the problem. Within days Mountbatten concluded that partition was inevitable and that it would have to be implemented as quickly as possible. By 3 June he had secured the agreement of the Indian leaders; the new dominions of India and Pakistan were to come into existence on 15 August. As the proposed partition line ran through the rich farmlands of the central Punjab, with its mixed population of Sikhs, Hindus and Muslims, an intensification of the slaughter was inevitable. A dual burden fell on Auchinleck. He had to maintain the good order and discipline of the army, the one force which could hope to contain the outbreaks of communal violence. At the same time he had to preside over its division. He was determined that from 15 August each dominion would have viable armed forces. This meant that predominantly Muslim units would be sent to Pakistan and non-Muslim units to India. For the rest of the armed forces, men would be allowed to choose which of the new dominions they wished to serve. Appropriate administrative machinery had to be established.[27]

All of this had to be attempted in a matter of weeks at a time when, in the Punjab at least, the situation was fast spiralling out of control. On 15 August Auchinleck assumed the new role of Supreme Commander of all armed forces in India and Pakistan. In an attempt to maintain peace, he set up the Punjab Boundary Force under General Rees which was to be directly responsible to him. The magnitude of his task became clear on the 14th when he flew to Lahore to consult with Rees and the departing Governor of the Punjab, Sir Evan Jenkins. As he flew over the Sikh holy city of Amritsar he could see that parts of the city and surrounding villages were burning. In Lahore some 15 per cent of the city had been destroyed, the police had collapsed and only the army was preventing a 'complete holocaust'. Such was the situation only twelve hours before the end of the British Raj. Impartiality was out of fashion. On 1 September the Punjab Boundary Force was dissolved and three weeks later Mountbatten, now Governor-General of an independent India, wrote in a sorrowful letter to Auchinleck that the government regarded his presence and role as a derogation of its sovereignty. It was notice to quit. Even so, at the end of October he used his continuing prestige and commonsense to help avert war between India and Pakistan over Kashmir. On 1 December 1947, refusing the peerage he had been offered, he left the country he had come to regard as home.

Auchinleck died in 1981 after a long and rather lonely retirement, latterly in Marrakech whose surroundings recalled the North-West Frontier of India. His Ulster links were renewed through his Colonelcy of the Inniskilling Fusiliers. Visitors to the regimental museum at Enniskillen may see mementoes of his forty years of service, including the battledress he wore during his historic battles in the summer of 1942. He was still visiting Ireland in the mid-1970s when he was over ninety. During these years he had the satisfaction of seeing his military reputation, which had suffered at the hands of Montgomery, steadily restored. In 1948 he had assured the military historian, Basil Liddell-Hart, that the truth would prevail in the end, and so it proved. He preferred to let the record speak for itself, refusing to write his memoirs or to be provoked by those of others. He was reticent about the desert campaigns but painstakingly generous to historians, like the present writer, who were interested in the affairs of his beloved India. By the late 1950s historians were confirming the decisive nature of his victory over Rommel at Alamein. Armed with the legacies of Britain's unpreparedness for war, it had been his fate to fight and beat a determined enemy at the full flood of his fortunes, only to see the credit go to others. This solitary Ulsterman had amply lived up to his Indian title of the 'Lord of War'. He asked for nothing more.

HELEN WADDELL

1889–1965

Scholar and Author

Felicitas Corrigan

HELEN WADDELL

> The art of writing has this at least in common with the kingdom of God — that it knows no frontiers: the wind blows where it lists, and you cannot tell whence it comes. But I like to think that what is bred in the bone comes out in the prose: and mine was bred in an old house in Down, on a 'rath' above the road that goes through Loughbrickland to the south. Swift must have ridden past it when he got his horse shod in Loughbrickland riding down to Dublin from Kilroot. No one ever came to it, and the trees had grown so close that the dark house saw nothing but its own deep well of a garden filled to the brim with sun. But from the rath the ground fell away to the Mournes: and on the west one saw the morning light lying like water on the green level fields of Armagh. The house was full of spent lights of green water, like the light wavering on the walls of a sea-cave: full too of the spent lights of living, for the casual reading of generations was there: and it was here I read *Wuthering Heights* and Charles O'Malley, and the thrillers of the seventies, and *Twelfth Night* in a pirated Dublin edition of Dr Johnson's Shakespeare, and the Apocrypha, and masses of seventeenth-century theology, and spent wakeful nights wrestling with predestination as with Apollyon, secure of my personal damnation: but forgot it all in the morning over a brown egg for breakfast.

None but Helen Waddell could have hoarded that youthful experience and, with her power of evocation and poetic imagination, transmuted it into patterns of thought and language in which the music of vowel and consonant, the rhythm of the cadences, and the creative richness are so essentially Irish. Her style has the subtle and convincing quality of her own resonant voice, that voice described by listeners as 'lovely and seductive', and by herself as resembling a grandfather clock, its deeper notes being the very thing to lead in prayer. At chanting pitch, it could reach the furthest end of a large lecture hall. The house that provided her with her land of faery was Ballygowan, a romantic two-storeyed building three centuries old, contemporary with the Westminster Assembly of Divines. Beautiful and dignified with age, it was Helen's dream that one day she would be its mistress after the death of the beloved spinster great-aunt and uncle with whom she spent her annual holidays; but when the time came, the house passed to another, and is now no more. During the First World War, Helen wrote four articles on Ballygowan for the *Manchester Guardian*. One of these, entitled 'Seisin' — the possession of land by freehold — expresses her inner attitude towards her homeland:

> The house is without principle: it has no politics; it has only passion. There are a few houses like it in Ulster, but the passion is born only of the fields. It is not of Belfast. Belfast is Unionist or Nationalist; Belfast has principle, principle and politics and loyalty. But these have no nationality; they have only a country ... They cleave to it with the possession that is nine points of the law and the tenth point of passion that outweights the nine. And so unwittingly they inherit by the oldest law of all. They have taken seisin of Ireland: they hold the square of turf.

The roots of Helen Waddell's patriarchal tree were in Scottish not Irish soil. 'We are originally alien stock', Helen wrote in a letter to her sister, Meg. 'But 300 years of Irish climate and Irish land have so profoundly modified us that we are no longer Scottish. We haven't a trace of it in looks even, and our language is English with the Irish idiom.' There had existed strong links between the two countries since the Stone Age. Separated by a mere strip of water, each settled in the other's territory as he would, in frequent and friendly exchange, as St Bede testifies. No country suffered so cruelly as Ireland from the invasions of the Northmen. Many a ninth-century Irishman took the road for the same reason that so many scholars are refugees in our own day, because they could no longer live in peace in their own country. As Helen was to remind some Irish schoolchildren, men's clothes change a good deal in a thousand years, but not their minds, and still less the things they do. Some of those Irish wanderers had more scholarship than sanctity, and some little of either: youthful revels are not a modern phenomenon; but as an exile who had tasted homesickness for Ballygowan and Kilmacrew, and knew by experience the destruction wrought by hatred and war, Helen was able very easily to identify herself with the Irish monks in flight from the Danes, who turned at the top of the hill at Bangor or Clonfert or Clonmacnoise to see the quiet roofs they knew flaring red to heaven, while the Northmen sacked the holy places. She knew exactly how one of them felt, when he searched in his satchel for his notebook and scribbled down:

My little house, my heart, 'twas God himself
  That thatched your roof.
And through the thatch no rain can fall,
  And no man fears
The sharp points of the spears
  And round the garden is no fence at all.

The Ostmen, as they were called, left a sad legacy of savagery and bloodshed to a people by nature noble and highly-gifted, but now far removed by vice from the decencies of civilized life. Perished from memory was the Golden Age of the sixth century when, to quote Helen Waddell's *The Wandering Scholars*, 'that fierce and restless quality, which had made the pagan Irish the terror of Western Europe, seemed to have emptied itself into the love of learning and the love of God.' Shiploads of scholars travelled by the old trade routes to Cork or Bangor, while Irishmen in their turn went out to found some of the most famous monastic strongholds of learning, wisdom and sanctity throughout Europe. In a letter to Meg, written in 1924, Helen describes her discovery of some of these countrymen. She had returned from Paris, true Irish wandering scholar as she was, and ploughing through manuscripts in the British Museum, in the hope of finding something that would bring to life a century that had a rather bad name, she was suddenly electrified:

> It's the Irish scholars on the Continent in the ninth century. How they've come alive for me, starting with a Sedulius Scottus (Scot means Irish in the Middle Ages), and Sedulius is Latin for Sheil! He came to be schoolmaster at Liege, and wrote verses, and a Greek text of St Paul's epistles with a Latin translation — but the names in the margin of the MS are Dubthach, and Fergus, and Comgan — and his own. And these same names occur in a Latin MS of Priscian now in the monastery of St Gall (founded by an Irishman in the sixth century -the most famous centre of learning in Europe) ... They don't know when it was written, maybe by Sedulius' fellow-monks before they came to Europe, but the marginal notes are 'A hot Easter Sunday', 'It's getting dark', 'I'm cold', 'Would you rather I went?' (which means a conversation in the scriptorium, just like schoolboys). 'Cairbre and I both come from Inchmadoc', and this that struck at my heart, all by itself, 'Nendrum on Mahee'. You remember. Think of it, somebody maybe in Liege or St Gall, suddenly remembering the peat. Then in odd corners of the MS are poems in Irish:
> "Bitter is the wind tonight: it tosses the ocean's white hair,
> I fear not the coursing of the clear sea by the fierce heroes from the Lochlann."
> Do you wonder it took me in the legs? And I got on the track of it almost guiltily, thinking it's Irish sentiment is wasting your time — and now it has made a whole rather dull century come alive.

By the twelfth century there was still a tolerable amount of internecine warfare between rival Irish chieftains but most of the invasions were over — except the one which was to have vast and violent repercussions to our own day. On 19 December 1154, in his twenty-first year, Henry Plantagenet, already by inheritance monarch of a third part of France, was crowned King of England at Westminster. Eloquent, affable and dignified, he was nevertheless a man of pride, passion, rapacity and boundless ambition. Next door to his realm he saw an island with splendid harbours and a wealth of timber, peopled by natives inferior in the art of war, however superior their talents on the harp. Possibly there was one valid consideration. Long years of savagery and bloodshed had undeniably led to a general decay of the habits and seemliness of human living. Outstanding contemporaries such as Lanfranc, Anselm, Bernard and, above all, St Malachy of Armagh (1095-1148) bear witness to Ireland's sorry plight. Malachy O'More, driven by his own people from Bangor to Lismore to Iveragh in Kerry and thence to Armagh, ended his life at Clairvaux, where he died in the arms of his friend, St Bernard, having failed to turn the wolves of his turbulent flock into sheep. Henry II's secret ambition decided that loss of independence and annexation to his crown would be a paltry price for the free and unoffending Irish to pay for the benefits of refinement, education, and the reform of their clergy. So he at once despatched his envoy to Rome, to lay his project of invasion before the English Pope, Adrian IV. It was planned, he said, in order to instruct an ignorant nation, to extirpate vice from the Lord's vineyard, and to extend the annual payment of Peter's Pence to Rome. Succeeding centuries have standardized this pattern of masking politics, ambition and war under cover of piety and religion. What Henry II began, Elizabeth I continued, and Oliver Cromwell completed: 'We refused them quarter', says Cromwell's despatch after the five-day massacre of Drogheda. 'I believe we put to the sword the whole number of the defendants ... This is a marvellous great mercy.' The fruits of this subjugation are with us still: national resentment, vengeance, death and loss of Eden. Once, when Helen Waddell was preparing a lecture entitled 'The Sense of the Past', an English friend remarked: 'Surely an odd choice for an Irish audience? I thought the trouble was that the Irish had too much sense of the past.' Helen replied: 'The trouble is rather that they remember tragedy but not its reconciling: the blinding of Gloucester and the madness of Lear, but not the final vision of the old king stripped of egotism and exalted by passion to the stature of the saints.' At this point, the reader may well wonder what such a historical summary has to do with Helen Waddell? By a stroke of dramatic irony, Henry II's envoy to Pope Adrian was none other than John of Salisbury, one of the most powerful inspirations of Helen's life.

Before the final subjugation of Ireland in 1653, many of the chieftains had gone into the service of Catholic powers abroad; any who remained retired with their men into bogs and fastnesses where they formed bodies of armed forces called Raparees and Tories — a word derived from the Gaelic *toruighim*, meaning 'to pursue for the sake of plunder'. Hounded as they were, the Irish fugitives were driven to make food forays to sustain life itself. The land was left desolate. But not for long. Scotsmen had always found a second home in Down and Antrim, but with the religious change of the sixteenth century the whole landscape of thought and sympathy had undergone profound change. No longer were hands stretched out in friendship across the narrow straits between Antrim and Argyll. England had become a Protestant country with an Episcopal church; in 1560 Scotland had opted for a Presbyterial form of church government, and in 1638 the Scottish Covenanters pledged themselves not only to resist the Laudian liturgy of Canterbury, but also to wipe out popery. In their search for the freedom and order of simple Presbyterian worship, the Scots found in Ulster a new America within a few hours from their shores where, instead of roaming Red Indians, bands of wild Tories lurked in bogs, woods and mountains, homeless and hungry, called for that reason 'the woodkernes'.

In two biographical 'Notes' that give no indication of where or to whom she spoke, Helen has sketched her ancestry; the stress on American associations suggests an audience in the U.S.A.:

> The original 'Grandfather William' of the family fought for the Covenant at Bothwell Brig in 1679, but escaped with his life; rode peaceably home, and when Claverhouse's dragoons came riding across the moors to take him a few days later, he baffled them by a trick that had more of Ulysses in it than of martyrdom: for the family tradition goes that he met them at his hall door with a courteous 'Gentlemen, you have ridden hard: you will be thirsty', and had them into a good meal and a better

drink: and when the whole company was snoring drunk above and below the table, went out into the yard, cut the tethers of the horses and sent them galloping over the bogs, while himself and his sons rode down to the coast and took ship for Ireland. One of these sons made an excellent marriage, and got as his wife's dowry eight townlands near Newry in County Down, a mile or so from the house where Patrick Bronte, father of Charlotte and Emily and Anne, was born; only two townlands are left to them now, but some of the names are there to this day.

My grandfather, Hugh Waddell, came from it to be minister in Glenarm, one of the Antrim glens: 'He was that well liked,' said an old woman to me, 'that if he had taken all that was offered him in one day in the Glens, he wouldn't ha' come home straight in the saddle.' He married Margaret, a sister of Captain Mayne Reid, author of *The Rifle Rangers* and *The Scalp Hunters* — I sat beside a man in the Paris Metro who was reading *The Rifle Rangers* in French, and they tell me he is very popular in Russia ... He was trapping on the Red River and the Missouri at twenty, held a commission in the American army, came back to Europe, settled down to novel-writing in London, made a fortune, and died a poor man. My father, his nephew, had his recklessness, tempered with a sanctity that was almost medieval; he went out as a pioneer missionary to Manchuria, and though the harshness of the climate drove him to a milder sky in Japan, he had a vast admiration for the Chinese till the day of his death, and was something of a sinologue, the Vicar of Wakefield turned Chinese scholar. He was profoundly, if absent-mindedly, attached to his family, and after each furlough he brought back with him to Japan as many of us as he could afford. It was the habit of our youth — the two brothers and two sisters who made up the tail of a family of ten — to discuss endlessly how many times each of us had been round the world. I, the least of them, cut a poor figure in these global calculations, with only one-and-a-half to my credit: and as the first voyage was at the unobservant age of one, my elders refused to count it. The

> last journey home was in the autumn of 1900, when my father was sixty and I eleven. In six months he was dead, with his manuscript, *The Interpretation of the Trinity to the Chinese Mind,* a mass of indecipherable notes, most of them in Chinese.
>
> It had been an enchanted childhood: four of us behind the great bamboo fence that shut in a landscape garden with mountains and a pond and a stone bridge and a lizard that George trained to go up one sleeve and across his back and down the other. But looking back, the creative memory to me is the murmur of my father's voice, he pacing up and down the verandah in the early light and the household still asleep; the Psalms in Hebrew, the New Testament in Greek, the Lord's Prayer in Japanese. I still have his backless one-volume Shakespeare, underlined and annotated for the discriminating uses of 'soul' and 'spirit' and 'mind'.

This neat biographical summary has omitted an important name, that of Mayne Reid's great-uncle, James Porter. It was characteristic of Helen Waddell to pass over in silence the experiences that lay closest to her heart. There were those who obviously moulded her thought from without, such as the academics, George Saintsbury and Gregory Smith; more potent by far was the hidden force that affected not merely outlook and action, but her very being. Sensitive as few are, she responded not only to the life around her, but to what A. E. (George Russell) praised as the profundities and illuminations and intensities of past ages. Close scrutiny of her word and action would suggest that she was in a kind of habitual communion with two very wise men: her eighteenth-century kinsman, James Porter, Presbyterian minister and Irish patriot; and the twelfth-century Englishman, John of Salisbury, secretary to the martyr, Thomas Becket, and later Bishop of Chartres. These two, with her own father, she regarded as the spirits of just men made perfect.

James Porter (1753-98), handsome, brilliant and ardent in sympathy like so many Irishmen, was licensed by the Presbytery of Bangor, and at the age of thirty-four received a call to Grey Abbey where he was ordained in 1787. Misery and discontent surrounded him, caused by exorbitant rents, eviction of tenants, and sweated labour. The cry of 'Liberty, Equality and Fraternity', reverberating throughout Europe, awakened answering echoes in an Ireland labouring under political and religious oppression. From pulpit and platform James Porter attacked abuses, wrote satirical ballads to catchy airs sung all over Donegal, and demanded freedom of conscience for every one of the '800,000 Northerners, insulted and reviled because they talk of Emancipation, Union and Reform.' Although deeply committed to the United Irishmen, James Porter had never taken the oath; but that could not save him from the implacable hatred of Lord Londonderry, whom he had often lampooned. With the advent of open rebellion in 1798, he was forced into hiding in the fourteen-mile stretch of cliffs and caverns of the Mourne mountains, but they could not conceal him for long — the price set on his head sharpened the noses of his pursuers. He was caught and sentenced to be hanged before his own manse door. 'His wife dragged herself and her children (she had eight, including a child at the breast) to plead for him ... At the last, dumb with agony, she came out to meet her husband as the grim procession came down the road. It halted to let him speak to her. He looked at her smiling. "So, dearest," he said, "I am to sleep at home tonight." It is one of the immortal stories,' Helen adds, 'savagery and treachery and pain flowering at the gallow's foot into high poetry.' She loved the Mournes with a possessive passionate love of home. There is a snapshot of her as a comely girl with an Irish smile, etched against sharp rocks beside a mountain stream gushing in a succession of waterfalls to the green Irish Sea below — one can almost hear the bees blundering among the white heather, the bog myrtle and the golden whins, the heart of heaven to James Porter's descendant:

> I shall not go to heaven when I die,
> But if they let me be,
> I think I'll take a road I used to know
> That goes by Shere-na-garagh and the sea.

And all day breasting me the winds will blow
And I'll hear nothing but the peewits' cry
And the waves talking to the sea below.

There is a tide in the affairs of men, a flux and ebb, a rhythmic recurrence, and in many ways James Porter's life was reflected in the lives of Helen and her father. In 1891 Hugh Waddell had sent his ailing wife and young children to Belfast, settling for economy's sake in lodgings in Tokyo. 'I remember sitting with him at supper', George Braithwaite, a fellow missionary recalled, 'and there was nothing on the table but bread, and water, and sometimes milk. There was not any butter. It was a hard life. But he was Irish to the last. I remember how he kept us laughing ... I saw, years ago, the crest taken by an Indian missionary: it was an ox, and the motto: "For service or for sacrifice." We say "The Lord is my shepherd", and it is a word of great comfort. But there is the other side. For why does the shepherd guard the sheep?' Not for nothing did James Porter and Hugh Waddell share the same blood: the torment of martyrdom is not restricted to the noble army of Church litanies.

'O Life, a road to life art thou, not Life. And there is no man makes his dwelling in the road, but walks there; and those who fare along the road have their dwelling in the fatherland.' These words of the sixteenth-century Irish Columbanus are a perfect summary of the lives of these countrymen of his, and of Helen Waddell who translated them. A deep-seated conviction of the necessity of suffering and negation, if life is to be whole surfaced constantly in all her writing. Her *Leitmotif*, loved and quoted beyond all other passages of Scripture — and how she knew her Bible! — came from Isaiah 38: 'O Lord, by these things men live, and in all these things is the life of the spirit.' The preceding verse is taken for granted: 'I shall go softly all my years in the bitterness of my soul.'

Born in 1889 and educated at Victoria College for Girls, Helen passed in 1908 to Queen's University, graduated with first-class honours, was awarded a research studentship that brought her into the ambit of European scholarship and medieval Latin; in addition, it gave her the enrichment of George Saintsbury's unique friendship; but for the rest she was forced along a stony path of asceticism with the domineering egoist of a stepmother, to whom she sacrificed her entire youth. 'Spirit must brand the flesh that it may live' — the 'lost decade' as she called it, gave Helen time to reflect, to descend within herself into a region of stress and strife, and to emerge with a profound, dispassionate knowledge of human nature inseparable, as John of Salisbury's theory and her forebears' practice taught her, from mystery and Divine truth. They were also years of astonishing productivity. Perched like a sparrow on the housetop of a tiny leaded roof outside her stepmother's bedroom window, she could forget the invalid's incessant moans and the radiating spokes of shabby streets, spawned by nineteenth-century town-planners for Harland & Wolff's employees; and, pen in hand, recapture the magic of Tokyo and her enchanted childhood in stories, reviews, essays, a play *The Spoiled Buddha* (1915) and, best known of all, her *Lyrics from the Chinese.* The death of her stepmother in 1920 set her free to go up to Somerville; in 1923 Lady Margaret Hall gave her the Susette Taylor Travelling Fellowship for two years. In 1927 *The Wandering Scholars* issued from the press, followed two years later by *Mediaeval Latin Lyrics;* and from then until the outbreak of the Second World War, every book she published enjoyed *un succes fou,* while its author became a celebrity, mixing with ease in the London salons with members of the British Cabinet, or sitting in 10 Downing Street talking to Queen Mary and Stanley Baldwin. So much for enrichment: was there also negation? Undoubtedly: her ear was ceaselessly attuned to the giant agony of the world; it found expression in a quotation from Goldsmith. She told Meg: 'It's still true, 'though you get all fizzy when things like this happen, it never seems to touch the inside of you:

> "Still to my brother turns with ceaseless pain
> And drags at each remove a lengthening chain."

You go up a hill when you're young ... and think you will go on walking into the westering sun. And then you find a precipice and a valley of dry bones — and if one looks for Him, I suppose, God.'

God had been her goal since childhood. She quoted the Bible with enviable ease; at the age of eight she knew *Hebrews* by heart, and would climb with bare toes up the knobbly trunk of a maple tree in the Tokyo garden to sit cradled in its boughs, cudgelling her brains over the meaning of resurrection and eternity. Later, during the 'lost decade', she gave weekly Bible talks and wrote prayers for the Girls' Auxiliary of Belfast. 'Could she make the prayers simpler, as they were for working girls?', she was asked. 'I did not change the prayer beginning "Thy eternity dost ever besiege our life" ... because by all means possible I wanted to hammer into the brain of your working-class girl some idea of eternity, if it were only the beauty of the word. For to get any conception of infinity is like taking the stone off the mouth of a well.' She found her own thirst assuaged when she discovered Boethius, Augustine of Hippo, and above all, John of Salisbury, and the scholars' religion of the Middle Ages, that swept it from the intellectual plane to the eternity of the things of the spirit.

Always affirmative and positive, Helen never shirked the concrete situation. Painfully aware of 'social conditions that we take for granted' and were iniquitous, she shared James Porter's deep compassion for the hungry and oppressed, whoever they might be. There is only one Holy Spirit, she would say, and He is no respecter of persons: heroism and holiness were to be found on both sides of the Great Divide. She extended her love equally to the little Methodist, Sadie Patterson, in 1918 left motherless at the age of twelve to cope with a family of eight children and an invalid stepfather, to work as her mother had done to earn 'Wages 16s.3d. for 50 doz. sheets and overalls, less 1s.0d. for thread'; or to the eldest of six from the Falls left fatherless at the age of eight: 'To think o' that craythur workin' in the mill since she was nine, glad to creep in to the warmth of a strange fire to end her days, like a harassed cat that the children has been tormentin', crawlin' under a dure-scraper to die in pace. It's terrible when ye think o' it.' Helen's biblical summing-up is typical: 'O Lord, by these things men live, and in all these things is the life of the spirit.' This same craving for justice and Christian brotherhood motivated her patriotism: politics smothered and dejected her. She lived through the Easter Rising of 1916. 'You know, the father of me before me was a passionate Home Ruler', she wrote to Dr Taylor, 'and upon my honour, scores of the men who died in Easter week died for a dream's sake ... I'd bitterly resent having this blessed and adorable North made an English shire. Remember the tradition among us, that one of us was hanged for treason in '98, and that the Governor of the Jail where he was hanged was a kinsman of his own.'

'Whoever he be that is willing to suffer for his faith, whether he be little lad or man grown, Jew or Gentile, Christian or Infidel, man or woman, it matters not at all: who dies for justice dies a martyre, a defender of the cause of Christ.' The speaker is John of Salisbury, Henry II's envoy to Pope Adrian IV — 'It was at my request that he gave Ireland in hereditary possession to the illustrious King Henry II of England', he writes in his *Metalogicon* — humanist and politician, academic and Ciceronian who, more than all others, formed Helen Waddell into a European scholar of international repute. He commands more entries in the index to *The Wandering Scholars* than all others; in 1928 Helen contributed a masterly essay on him to the papers of The English Association; the full-scale biography that she planned was brought to nothing by the Second World War. It is not difficult to see affinities between master and disciple. When little more than a boy, hungry and penniless, John had found his way to Paris where he stood on Mont S. Genevieve, greedy for every word that fell from the lips of Peter Abelard. After twelve years of wandering through 'the divers cities of sweet France', he returned to England, a classical scholar who stood head and shoulders above all his contemporaries, to fritter away the next twelve years in the service of Church and State, 'I that had set my heart on things far other'. How often Helen was to quote those last words when World War II with its editorial chores in Constable's office, its doodlebugs and food shortages sapped physical strength and intellectual powers. There was no need for John to inform her that there was something in rhyming Latin that satisfied the ear of the world — she had discovered that for herself at the age of nine, when listening to three lines of Latin poetry quoted in *Uncle Tom's Cabin;* but he did impress on her lessons she never forgot: 'Words should be gently handled,' he admonished, 'not tortured like captive slaves, to make them give up what they never had.' Rarely did master have more apt disciple, for John's Prologue to his *Polycraticus* — on the vanity of the Court — might be an actual summary of Helen's wandering scholars and desert fathers and medieval lovers, who all communicate so powerfully the felt life of ordinary men and women: 'The dearest fruit of literature is this, that every grievous gulf of space and time annulled, it brings a man face to face with his friends.' It has a mysterious sweetness this setting of the mind's edge to the reading or writing of something that has worth. The country men inhabit it inside as well as outside, and both John of Salisbury and Helen Waddell had descended far enough into the inner darkness to reach those hidden springs of the past, that gave life to the present and vision to the future: 'In every darkness God has his stars, but to no purpose are great deeds done unless they take fire in the light of letters.'

But for Helen as for her mentor the day came when the hand lost its cunning, the minds its swift apprehension, the memory its fidelity. As John wrote in dejection:

> The years take all away, aye, even the soul.
>   The voice has fled the singer: all is fled.

In 1947, making an almost superhuman effort, Helen delivered the eighth W. P. Ker Memorial lecture in Glasgow with all her old magnetism and fire, but her letters at the time show that she knew she was standing before a precipice in the valley of dry bones, and God alone remained. The inexorable advance of Alzheimer's disease would gradually reduce her brilliant mind to a *tabula rasa,* blank and withdrawn — was the memorable passage towards the end of Peter Abelard prophetic?

> He saw the heavens opened: he saw no Son of Man. For a moment it seemed to him that all the vital forces in his body were withdrawing themselves, that the sight had left his eyes and the blood was ebbing from his heart: he felt the grey breath of dissolution, the falling asunder of body and soul. For a moment his spirit leapt towards heaven in naked adoration ... with no passion of devotion, but with every power of his mind, with every pulse of his body, he worshipped God.

Helen died in London on 5 March 1965. Her body was taken home to Ireland and laid beside her mother and grandmother beneath a long grey gravestone hewn from the rock that shapes the mountains of Mourne, in the parish churchyard of Maherally.

'To what purpose is this waste?' Helen's sister, Meg, asked in anguish. But Helen had answered that very question in 1917, in her *Memory of Meta Fleming* for the Girls' Auxiliary of Belfast:

> To what purpose is this waste? The end is not yet. One comes back to the wisdom of the Middle Ages — *Mors janua vitae,* Death the gate of Life. We believed in the life everlasting, but into the life everlasting we have come to read the life eternal, life infinite in its breadth and length and height and depth. For to know the will of God was not Paul's ultimate asking. It began "with the knowledge of His will"; it ended "with all the fullness of God".

In his *Metalogicon* John of Salisbury defines the Catholic *sanctus* as 'that which is made fast, the souls who have escaped the perpetual flux of vanity and now inhabit truth.' Would it be too much to apply this title to Helen Jane Waddell?

Born one hundred years ago, not in the bustling busyness of Belfast but in the Far East in Tokyo, a city at that time of wooden houses, lotus flowers and pungent pines, her life and character are something of a paradox. To the core of her being she was an Irish Presbyterian, sprung from a long line of Presbyterian clerical forebears, 'founded on the rock beneath the green pastures of Down but lifted up to be aware of far horizons', as she said of her brother-in-law, John Dunwoodie Martin. To this, her birth and upbringing added deep Asian sympathies too often overlooked — she interpreted the fourth-century Ausonius (A.D.310-95), dallying with anagram and compliment, in terms of the Chinese poet Po Chu-i of four centuries later — and the whole was finally leavened and permeated with Catholic devotion: 'I'll never be a Catholic', she told her sister, 'but I'd never get my work done if I didn't now and then dive into that strange divine sea'. These very qualities make her a commanding figure: she stands at a crossroads where time and place and eternity meet. Is she to face as in childhood what John of Salisbury calls 'that hostile and faithless stepmother to memory, Oblivion?'. Or will she remain 'Ulster's Darling'?

JOHN
LAVERY
1856–1941
Painter

Kenneth McConkey

JOHN LAVERY

There is a wavering, hesitant line to be drawn between biography and the kind of monograph favoured by art historians. The viewpoint often expressed is that artists are their work; and that their lives only provide incidental illumination to the pictures they paint. A biography which fails to take account of the artist's *oeuvre* is a peculiarly pointless exercise, concentrating upon what, by the most important set of measures, are a series of inconsequentials. In the case of Sir John Lavery, it is true that his life touched upon many of the most important lives of his day. He mixed with all strata of society, despite his very humble beginnings. He painted monarchs, statesmen, members of the aristocracy, as well as peasants in the field. He attained excellence in a profession where true distinction was readily recognized by the international community. Yet Lavery also lived at an exciting time when art was grappling with new styles and concepts. Initially he was in the vanguard of this activity and, although he was quickly overtaken, it was recognized at the time of his death that he had been 'one of the last of a great tradition, when the artist linked his art to what had gone before and thus led on with his own art to the art to come.'[1] Considering his sixty years of productive life as a painter, it is difficult not to be daunted by Lavery's immense industry. His descendants recall that he painted every day and that much of his restlessness was a consequence of the constant search for visual stimulus. Many of his best pictures were impromptu sketches, although this does not take anything away from more studied works like *The Tennis Party* and *The Bridge at Grez*. This short biography, therefore, can only hope to provide an introduction to a life and art which was intensely lived and produced.

Lavery was born in Belfast in 1856, the son of an unsuccessful publican. When he was aged three, his father perished *en route* for the United States. His mother died shortly afterwards and young Lavery was consigned to his uncle's farm near Moira. He remained there until, at the age of ten, he was dispatched to a relative at Saltcoats in Ayrshire, where he spent the remainder of his youth. In his late teens he made several unsuccessful attempts to find work in Glasgow before securing regular employment with the photographer, J. B. McNair. Lavery began to take art instruction at the Haldane Academy in 1875, and within three years had abandoned the photographic studio in order to become a painter. He was single-minded in his pursuit of this new career, to the extent that he refused to support his sister, Jane, when she fell on hard times. So precarious was his profession that Lavery instantly recognized that, with no family support, it would be necessary to paint whatever the market would accept. Accordingly his first works were costume-pieces bearing titles such as *The Courtship of Julian Peveril* and *Her First Disappointment.*

From the outset Lavery was fortunate in that the city of his adoption was experiencing the prosperity which goes with rapid industrial expansion. Glasgow, because of its ancient rivalry with Edinburgh, saw itself as a place where the arts could flourish. Its industrialists, as well as taking an intelligent interest in modern French painting, were keen to patronize young west of Scotland painters. In this ambiance Lavery enthusiastically developed his understanding of *avant-garde* Parisian styles and, after an unsuccessful winter in London at Heatherley's art school, he set off for Paris in 1881. There, in addition to producing costume studies for the Glasgow picture trade at the Atelier Colarossi, Lavery also joined the Academie Julian. This popular studio run by the successful Salon painters, Tony Robert-Fleury and William-Adolphe Bouguereau, was a seed-bed for the most radical thinking in the visual arts. Its masters were no more than mentors and, although he went to Julian's in awe of Bouguereau, Lavery quickly realized that the most innovative painting of his day was the modern naturalism of Jules Bastien-Lepage. Important modern life subjects such as *After the Dance* gave way to *plein air* pictures painted on the banks of the Marne at Nogent. It was with one of these, *Les Deux Pecheurs,* that he achieved his first success at the Parish Salon in 1883.

It was at this time that Lavery heard about the artists' colony at Grez-sur-Loing. In this tiny village a few miles south of Fontainebleau an international group of *plein air* painters had been congregating regularly since 1875. The initial attraction of the village for Lavery lay in the fact that it had spawned some of the best of recent paintings. In previous years painters like William Stott of Oldham and Louis Welden Hawkins had won medals for pictures painted at Grez. Lavery followed the well-worn paths to the river bank and embarked upon an ambitious picture of the ancient bridge, showing a young man in a punt calling to two women in a distant rowing-boat. The picture was initially entitled *A Passing Salute* although it became more popularly known as *The Bridge at Grez.* There is a similar feeling of indolence and summer idyll in the tiny picture, *A Grey Summer's Day, Grez.* These two works sum up Lavery's reaction to the village. In later years he confessed that the happiest moments of his life were spent at the artists' colony there.

Yet despite the indolent atmosphere, Lavery returned to Grez in 1884 with a serious programme of work. Influenced by the modern naturalism of the Salon he produced a large painting of a peasant washerwoman and child by the banks of the Loing speaking to a passing boatman, entitled initially *An Afternoon Chat,* but now known as *Under the Cherry Tree.* Again the focus of attention was social exchange rather than rural labour. This feature of Lavery's work was extended in other pictures such as *Sewing in the Shade* and *The Return from Market.* On several occasions the painter turned his attention to other members of the colony, painting male and female colleagues at work. One of these shows Mouat Loudan at work on a picture of the main street at Grez, while another is reputed to represent his Irish comrade, Frank

O'Meara.

Lavery was back in Glasgow by the end of 1884. During the next five years an informal group of painters was formed, in which he was the central character. The focal point of initial discussion amongst what were to be known as the 'Glasgow Boys' was Lavery's ambitious picture *The Tennis Party,* which was begun at Cartbank in the spring of 1885. It shows the *nouveaux riches* woollen manufacturers of Paisley, Lavery's first patrons, indulging in the newly fashionable game of lawn tennis. Following the French manner, Lavery began a small oil sketch in which the essential format of the composition was established. Like *The Bridge at Grez,* this was to be a frieze-like picture in which the estabishment of the *mise-en-scene* depended as much upon the strategic placing of the spectators as upon the players. The work excited the curiosity of Lavery's fellow painters, who watched its progress, and when it appeared at the Paris Salon George Moore hailed it as a 'work of real talent'. What was so surprising about a picture of the opulent middle classes at play?

Much of the *avant-garde* debate during the previous two decades concerned the portrayal of modern life. For French-trained painters like Lavery it was necessary to be of one's time, to abandon history painting and devote one's energies to the contemporary scene. Accordingly, when he completed his large Mary, Queen of Scots compositions, Lavery was looking for further opportunities to record real events which affected the lives of his fellows. In this respect his main chance came in 1888 with the staging of the Glasgow International Exhibition. Here was a focus for the display of wealth and power which would rival those of Manchester and Edinburgh in the previous two years. Temporary buildings were erected along the banks of the Kelvin to house displays from all over the Empire. Not satisfied with exhibiting his last history picture, *Dawn after the Battle of Langside,* the gregarious painter regularly re-visited the site to produce oil sketches of the crowds, the exhibits and the military tattoo. Forty of these small oils were displayed at a special show in Glasgow in October 1888.

One of the series was destined to become more famous than the others. This portrayed the state visit of Queen Victoria to the International Exhibition on 22 August 1888. Soon after the momentous event Lavery received a commission to enlarge his sketch into a grand commemorative group portrait containing over two hundred studies of individual participants. The credibility of the project depended, to some extent, upon the acquiescence of the Queen herself. Lavery was initially supplied with other portraits from which to copy a likeness, but he insisted that these were not good enough for his purpose. Various members of the entourage tried to help, but only after Prince Henry interceded on his behalf was he recalled to Windsor for a single sitting. The Queen appeared wearing the bonnet she had worn in Glasgow and, while she conversed with her ladies-in-waiting about flannel underclothing, Lavery sketched feverishly. After twenty minutes she left the room without showing any interest in the painter's results. Nevertheless, after this event the project was, in Lavery's words, 'plain sailing'. Sitters lined up to be included, but even then, transposing many small sketches to a large canvas was arduous and time-consuming. When the result was exhibited in Glasgow and London at the end of 1890, critical opinion was favourable.

One other event during the two years Lavery was at work upon the canvas had equally lasting effects. While painting politicians he used a studio in London borrowed from an old student friend, William Patrick Whyte. Coming out of an artists' colour shop in Regent Street one day he spotted a young flowerseller of such beauty that, upon impulse, he asked her to let him paint her portrait. Thereafter Kathleen MacDermott became his model, travelling to Glasgow with him. However, since her health was poor, she spent the first two months of 1890 with a married sister, returning, against his advice, to Lavery's studio in March. Finding her irresistible, with Whyte and Joseph Crawhall as witnesses, he married her. Their life together lasted barely a year, she dying of tuberculosis shortly after the birth of their only child, Eileen.

The emotional stress generated by these sad developments, coupled with the excitement of a major commission, necessitated a break from the busy round of activities in Glasgow. Lavery spent the early months of 1891 in Tangier, savouring for the first time the rich colour of Arab culture. Morocco had been recommended to him by other Glasgow painters like Melville and Crawhall and, although he was on holiday, the artist busily occupied himself with studies of the city and its immediate environs. Quickly framed after his return, these canvases formed the basis of his first London exhibition at the Goupil Gallery. Lavery's work was now increasingly recognized as a richly toned, 'voluptuous sort of impressionism'. Having gained a reputation in Paris, he was also being feted with other members of the Glasgow school in Munich. Tangier, regarded as a successful exploit, drew him back in subsequent years and, eventually, he bought a house there. His *oeuvre* in the mid-nineties contains interesting diversity. The romantic colour of Moorish dancers and snake-charmers contrasts with the restrained full-length portraits of great maturity. Comparisons were frequently made with Whistler and Velazquez, and to some extent these different aspects of his experience were conflated in the *Portrait of R. B. Cunninghame Graham*.

The bankrupt Scottish laird recalled that his first meeting with the painter occurred in Tangier when he stopped Lavery's runaway horse. It is indicative of his social aspirations that Lavery had been taking riding lessons in 1890, but by 1892 he was clearly no match for the former gaucho. Cunninghame Graham was larger than life. In former existences he had been a cattle rancher and a fencing instructor before taking his seat in Parliament. Although his efforts to restore the family fortune were mostly ineffectual, his commanding presence drew from Lavery one of his most famous images. George Bernard Shaw, who used him as the model for Captain Brassbound, summed him up as '... a Spanish hidalgo, hence the superbity [sic] of his portrait by Lavery (Velazquez being no longer available)'.

It was evident, however, that Glasgow provided a limited

number of such challenges. By 1896 Lavery had decided to move to London, not so much for its clientele as to be able to satisfy the international appetite for his work. He existed for two years in a borrowed studio before purchasing 5 Cromwell Place, the former home of the pre-Raphaelite painter, John Everett Millais. During these years up to the turn of the century he was as much in Rome and Berlin as London and Glasgow. The Munich, Berlin, Venice and Rome showings of his work were now bearing fruit in lucrative portrait commissions from European industrialists and members of the aristocracy. In Germany Lavery's friendship with the Westphalian painter, August Neven du Mont, was especially important since du Mont's wife, a member of the von Guilleaume dynasty of Cologne industrialists, supplied important patrons. Neven du Mont also introduced Lavery to one of his best known models, Mary Auras, who for five or six years around the turn of the century acted as a beautiful camp-follower. In 1898 Lavery visited the United States as a juror for the first international exhibition at the Carnegie Institute in Pittsburg. His important early work, *The Bridge at Grez,* was acquired by the Institute at this show. Other notable acquisitions followed and by 1904 he was the only living British painter to have two major works in the Musee du Luxembourg, the French modern collection.

Despite this undoubted success, Lavery did not get into the important London exhibitions. The year of his move from Glasgow saw his rejection from the Royal Academy and his subsequent refusal to exhibit there. This was more than compensated for by the role he came to occupy in the International Society of Sculptors, Painters and Gravers which he helped to form in 1898. Acting as the Society's Vice-President under Whistler and Rodin, Lavery's prominence was obviously enhanced. Both distinguished Presidents kept their distance from the business aspects of the Society, although, particularly in Whistler's case, there was a general oversight of its affairs. Lavery was particularly relied upon for his diplomatic skills.

In 1904, on a visit to Concarneau, an event occurred which

was to change Lavery's life. On the hotel verandah he noticed two American girls, Dorothy and Hazel Martyn, and their mother. Despite the fact that she had a suitor in attendance, Hazel was already engaged to be married to a Canadian doctor. Lavery was, nevertheless, struck by her natural elegance and resolved to keep in touch. When at the end of the following year he learned that Hazel was married, widowed and had been left with a baby daughter, he made a number of visits to Paris to renew their friendship. The fact that both were single parents drew them closer together and in 1910 they were married at Brompton Oratory.

Hazel instantly took to the life of the wife of an internationally renowned portraitist. The marriage, for instance, co-incided with a major retrospective of Lavery's work at the Venice Biennale. Many of his most important recent works, including the two from the Musee du Luxembourg, were shown to great acclaim. The consequence of this recognition was that the Royal Academy belatedly invited Lavery to join its ranks, and from 1911 onwards he became a regular exhibitor. To underline his eminence, a monograph on his work by Walter Shaw Sparrow was published in 1911, and a further retrospective was staged at the Grosvenor Galleries, London three years later. Lavery now had his own private secretary, and Hazel supervised the extensive socializing which occurred at their houses in London and Tangier.

In these years just before the Great War, the painter received a number of interesting and unusual commissions, one of which came from the publisher Hugh Spottiswoode. Lavery had already painted his wife and daughter, but on this occasion Spottiswoode requested a portrait of the Royal Family at Buckingham Palace, to be presented to the National Portrait Gallery. Working from studies produced at the Palace Lavery hurried to complete the picture for the opening of the Royal Academy in 1913. Before this happened the King and Queen visited Cromwell Place for a private preview. So enthused were they that, as Lavery recalled, the King wished 'to have a hand in it'. The painter dutifully mixed some royal blue which his majesty could apply to the Garter ribbon in the picture.

When in 1919 he completed one of his few religious works, *The Madonna of the Lakes*, a large triptych for St Patrick's Church in Belfast, he presented a study for *The Royal Family* ... to his native city, 'to show the other side that I was not a bigot.'

Among the many *habitues* of Lavery's studio around this time was the young Winston Churchill. Being temporarily out of a job in the early months of 1915, Churchill gave sittings for no less than four portraits. The experience was of more than usual significance as a learning exercise for the sitter, because when he took up painting more seriously in the early 'twenties at Cap Ferrat, Lavery was on hand to give tuition. However, more immediately, there was a war to be fought and, although he was now approaching sixty, the painter was anxious to employ his skills in recording the efforts of his fellow-countrymen. Returning from Dublin in August 1914 he went immediately to St James's Park, which had been transformed into a military camp, and there he produced one of the first war paintings. Although Hazel was fretful of any involvement with the hostilies, Lavery harboured a secret desire to equip a motor-van and head off for the Western Front. His opportunity came in 1917 when he was appointed one of the first official war artists. Initially, on account of his years, Lavery was assigned to painting munitions factories and naval bases, but his enthusiasm eventually led to his setting off in an airship to monitor North Sea convoys off Scapa Flow. On this occasion he produced what were among the first airborne oil studies for a large picture entitled *A Convoy, North Sea, 1918, From NS7*. Despite the originality of some of these scenes, Lavery came to disparage his war work, thinking that he saw in the horror and danger only new and exciting abstract arrangements. It was nonetheless true that his work revealed aspects of the war which were not generally appreciated, and it was to some extent in cognizance of this achievement that he was knighted in the New Year's Honours List in 1918.

Lavery returned from his war exploits to the recognition that during his absence there had been an upsurge of Irish nationalism.

He had begun to take an interest in art politics in Ireland around the turn of the century when he returned to regular exhibiting at the Royal Hibernian Academy. He was one of the Irish artists whose work was displayed at Hugh Lane's celebrated Guildhall exhibition in 1904, and again he represented Ireland at the Franco-British exhibition of 1908. It was Hazel, however, who encouraged a deeper involvement with the cultural renaissance taking place in Dublin in the years prior to the war, and she who encouraged their summer visits for the Horse Show and other social events. As leading London-Irish figures they were uniquely placed in the years after the war to make known their views on Irish affairs. They consorted with all of the leading politicians and there was even talk that Lavery might make a good Viceroy. Initially he sought sittings from Edward Carson and John Redmond on the strict condition that both permitted their pictures to hang side by side in the Dublin Municipal Gallery. Carson favoured Redmond's portrait, interpreting its quality as an expression of the painter's own political leanings. Redmond confined himself to the simple remark that he had always entertained the idea that 'Carson and I might some day be hanged side by side in Dublin ...'. While the negotiations for the Irish Treaty were going on in 1921 the Laverys played host to all of the protagonists, in return for portrait sittings. Of all the members of the Irish delegation, Michael Collins was the most romantic; the painter observed that he would only give sittings if he could be facing the studio door. The Laverys were back in Ireland after the signing of the Irish Treaty to witness the civil war in which Collins lost his life. A loyal supporter, Lavery went to the mortuary chapel to paint a final tribute to the dead leader, emotively inscribed 'Love of Ireland'.

During the inter-war years the painter strengthened his ties with his country of origin. He was elected President of the Belfast Art Society in 1919 for a five-year term, and when in 1930 the Ulster Academy of Arts was formed he was invited to act as President. During these years his visits to the north of Ireland were more frequent and he renewed his family ties with the Laverys of Moira. Both he and Hazel were amazed and honoured when in 1927 he was asked to provide a portrait of his wife, posing as Kathleen ni Houlihan, for use on the Free State currency. The image was engraved and in 1928 the first of the new notes appeared. Such was their popularity that they remained in circulation until 1975. Lavery's ties on both sides of the Border were now so strong that he contemplated making substantial donations of his work to both Irish capitals. In 1929 the newly opened Belfast Museum and Art Gallery received a collection of over thirty works, from all periods of the artist's career and some, like the *Twelfth of July, Portadown, 1928,* were specifically created for the occasion. In order to demonstrate the balance of his affiliations he visited Lough Derg in 1929 to paint a large picture of St Patrick's Purgatory. He had hoped for a harsh image of peasants plodding through the wind and rain, but was surprised to find that the pilgrims were 'everyday types', and the weather, being surprisingly good, gave the scene the air of a holiday resort.

In the 'twenties Lavery's career blossomed in other directions. Since about 1910 he had been painting what became known as 'portrait interiors'. A well-known artist, writer, or member of the aristocracy was to be seen in the disarray of their daily surroundings in what was often no more than a quick sketch. These works were drawn together for an exhibition in London in 1925 which was taken up by Sir Joseph Duveen, and which toured through five cities in the United States. The Laverys accompanied the show to New York and, while there, a number of portraits were produced. So successful was the venture that a further exhibition was staged at Palm Beach in 1928, and again the Laverys were in attendance.

Lavery returned to London in 1929 to another major commission: to paint the Court reception of King George V and Queen Mary, a massive group portrait similar to that with which his career had begun. The numerous studies for this were shown at a special exhibition at Colnaghi's in London in 1931. For the next few years Lavery's career was somewhat eclipsed by the declining health of his wife. In 1934 Hazel's condition dramatically deteriorated and she died at the beginning of the following year. *The Times* described her as a 'beautiful, popular, socially gifted and devoted wife', the perfect complement to a husband who was 'modest and retiring'. Fate then dealt a cruel blow. Within six months his only daughter, Eileen, by then Lady Sempill, was also dead and he was thrown more upon the support of his step-daughter, Alice, his granddaughter, Ann, and his new secretary, Katharine FitzGerald. Despite his own advanced years he set off, like Ulysses, to seek a new world. Fascinated by the young people's talk of Hollywood, he decided to go there and paint the stars. He made two winter visits to America, one of which was at the request of Gertrude Coutts. This too ended in tragedy. Returning from a restaurant in the desert, the party was involved in a car crash and Mrs Coutts, who in a fine operatic voice had been treating them to a rendering of Ave Maria, was killed. Lavery's last ambition was only partly realized. There were portraits of Shirley Temple, Maureen O'Sullivan and Loretta Young, but the idea of a great canvas executed in the film studio, while the sets were changing and shooting was going on, was abandoned.

With an air of finality, Lavery enlisted the help of John Steward Collis and John Masefield to help record his memoirs which were published in 1940, but realizing that London was no place for him in wartime he went to stay with Alice at her home in Kilkenny. While contemplating a summer programme of painting, he died there on 10 January 1941.

CHARLES GAVAN DUFFY

1816-1903

Rebel and Statesman

Gerard O'Brien

CHARLES GAVAN DUFFY

Few Victorian statesmen met with such success as did Charles Gavan Duffy in attempting to pre-empt history's verdict on them. A useful but overall rather indifferent smattering of letters and papers were left to posterity, but their usefulness was reduced by the failure of most of his contemporaries to leave similar collections in their wake. The inevitable result was that Duffy's own writings became, and have remained almost exclusively, the principal source for the behind-the-scenes politics, strategies and general affairs of the Young Irelanders. The extent to which Duffy spoiled things in a sense for later commentators is suggested by the absence of a full-length scholarly study of the Young Ireland movement until as late as 1986. Historians, indeed, moved in on Duffy only gingerly and obliquely, visiting one and then another of the various movements with which he was associated, and withholding a proper biographical treatment until almost all other avenues had been explored.

For historians of Ireland (and Irish-born historians in particular) Duffy's life was not an easy one to come to grips with. Having been a multi-faceted life, it contravened and even existed outside the normal rules of play which traditionally are supposed to have governed the lives of Irish nationalists. If one begins life as an extremist, as Duffy did, one is not expected to become a constitutionalist, as Duffy did. If one begins one's political journey as a separatist, as Duffy did, one is not expected to become a supporter of imperialism, as Duffy did. Yet for all these outward signs of political apostasy, Duffy was rarely accused of treachery during his own lifetime and, even more amazingly, he has not become one of the 'villains' of Irish history. The nationalist mantle of odium fell for a time with far less justification on Daniel O'Connell; and with far greater intensity on John Sadleir and William Keogh who were too human in their weakness.

In all treatments of the various movements in which Duffy had a prominent or even controlling role there is an undercurrent of awareness that Duffy was a larger-than-life figure, one who defied categorisation and so must be left to one side for an ever-lengthier moment. Duffy himself was conscious of the difficulties, and his autobiography divided his life into one spent 'in two hemispheres'. His most recent biographer has added a third 'life' — that spent in Nice chronicling his past experiences. Duffy was keenly aware of the changes in direction and sometimes of attitude which life had forced on him, but he would admit of no fundamental inconsistency. On his retirement from Australian politics in 1880 he still believed that 'unfinished designs of early life might be taken up and completed — for work which did not aim to serve Ireland had no attraction for me'. For Duffy, it is clear, the various strands which traversed his life, however tangled they may have become, remained unbroken at the finish, and were possessed of a strength and endurance which defied all attempts to sever them. Most of all they have defied all efforts by historians to ascertain their true nature. It is time to take one further look at these strands.

With regard to Duffy's early life we are rather too dependent for comfort upon his own testimony. However, that testimony on occasion revealed between its lines aspects of Duffy's character unsuspected by the man himself. For instance, Duffy's efforts to depict himself as a fully-fledged member of a down-trodden people are not borne out by the facts, some of which he himself quotes. Duffy's background was ineffably Catholic and of unusual prosperity. His mother's father was the leaseholder of 'a large tract of land ... and was in fact a gentleman farmer'. His father's forebears likewise had been leaseholders of sufficient prominence to allow their acceptance as suretors for 'a dozen priests of Clogher'. The pedigree was lent added respectability by the fact that the Clogher clergy of his boyhood years included 'half a dozen' related Duffys. Duffy himself arrived in 1816 as the fortunate scion of a Monaghan town shopkeeper 'who ... had accumulated considerable property in houses and townparks', and who moreover owned a share in a prosperous bleach-green.

At the time of his father's death, when Duffy was ten, his elder brothers were pursuing the almost classical Catholic apprenticeships in trade and medicine. The younger Duffys passed into the guardianship of a related priest and their lives under the management of their widowed mother. In line with the experience of his Catholic contemporaries and forebears, Duffy's earliest education was obtained in a local hedge-school, conducted in this instance by a benevolent but ill-equipped one-armed man. Duffy referred to his 'escape' from this establishment as 'one of the most fortunate incidents of my life'. A strong-willed elder sister, catching sight of Duffy one day in the midst of his peasant schoolmates, plucked him thence and forbade him to return. The often-overlooked importance of status over religion in nineteenth-century Ulster society was manifested in the decision to send young Duffy to the non-Catholic classical academy run by the Reverend John Bleckley in Monaghan town. Duffy was the first and, in his time, the only Catholic at the school, but this was the mid-1820s and for more than a generation Catholics had been gradually making 'first appearances' in hitherto exclusively Protestant domains.

But the place was Monaghan; history and demography coalesced to make Duffy's education a quintessentially Ulster experience. Writing near the end of his life, Duffy was conscious that the Ulster environment and related experiences were a formative influence on him. Reading material of an historical character was, not surprisingly, scarce, but Duffy lived not far from places from which Catholics had been forcibly driven during the disturbances of the 1790s. In his youth 'the Orange drum was heard on every hill from June to August to celebrate the Boyne and Aughrim'. During one procession he witnessed the murder of a Catholic butcher 'by a Government gun'. He had 'never seen a history of Ireland' but, he wrote, 'there was a history transacted under our eyes of which it was impossible to be ignorant'. As a prosperous Catholic he was keenly aware of power structures and status differentials which would have been mysteries or irrelevant to the less materially blessed of his co-religionists. His five years at Bleckley's academy, however, proved valuable not only for the sound academic education that Duffy received there, but also because they helped him to relate to Protestants and Presbyterians in a way which would never be learned by many Catholics even of his own class.

Duffy's initial choice of career was determined partly by his background and circumstances, but partly also by the chance encounters that cast him at an impressionable age amongst journalists. Because of the religious tests then in force his guardian refused to send him to Trinity College. Through a family acquaintance, Charles Teeling of '98 fame, Duffy became involved in promoting the proposed publication of the *Northern Herald,* a nationalist paper to which he soon began to contribute prose and verse. Moreover, he had relations in the profession. A powerful influence was Duffy's cousin, T. M. Hughes, then the Dublin correspondent for the *Morning Chronicle.* With his guardian's consent Duffy was taken on as a 'tyro' or unpaid trainee by the *Morning Register,* a paper which had its origins in the Catholic emancipation campaign of the 1820s. Life in Dublin, however, failed to live up to its romantic reflection in distant Monaghan. The capital's newspaper world would appear to have been run by a combination of cynics, hacks and freelance layabouts. Daniel O'Connell, when Duffy finally came within viewing distance of him, 'proved the great disillusionment'. The great man, considered Duffy, bore little resemblance to O'Neill, Sarsfield and Grattan. Even allowing for the distance in time at which Duffy recorded these impressions, it seems clear that his early disappointing experiences in Dublin encouraged in him the tendency to reject the mundane in favour of the romantic, and to prefer theatrical violence to undramatic constitutional politics. 'The panorama of

Irish resistance', he later wrote, '...passed before my imagination, and I burned to strike a blow in that hereditary conflict'.

Motivated by a growing need to escape the arduous life on the daily *Register*, of which he had been made an editor, and moved perhaps also by a desire to 'strike a blow' among his Ulster roots, Duffy accepted an editorial post on the *Vindicator*. This was a bi-weekly paper of Catholic inspiration based in Belfast and within a few months Duffy became its owner. It was of course through journalism that Duffy made his most indelible long-term mark on Irish history. His role was assured not only by his background, training and natural abilities, but also by the time in which he lived. Journalism in Ireland dated back to the seventeenth century, but mass readership was a product of nineteenth-century circumstances. O'Connell had already made effective use of the limited literacy that had prevailed in the countryside in his heyday. While it is not certain that Duffy in 1839-40 fully appreciated the implications of the National School system for popular literacy, time would show him to be one of its principal beneficiaries. In its content and general approach the *Vindicator* was the precursor to the *Nation*.

Like his education and his career, Duffy's direction in politics was determined partly by his background and, not least, by his temperament. He was a Catholic of Irish lineage, heir, as he believed it, to a political pedigree which based itself on resistance to the English invader. He was an educated Ulsterman, keenly aware of the politico-religious divisions in Irish society and of the advantage afforded by them to the old enemy. Moreover, Duffy was an early Victorian, one of the lower middle class who had not yet grown too numerous to be kept from rising socially within their own generation. In one of his earliest encounters with Irish nationalist literature he noted that the Irish forces in 1798 had been led by 'an Irish gentleman'. Duffy's involvement with nationalism may have been pervasive, but it was not all-pervading. He retained sufficient grasp of the practicalities (at least in the earlier days) to rise rapidly from reporter to editor to owner. His one shift in a leftwards direction when he formed an embryonic press association in 1838 was experimental and brief. When the moment came in 1842 to establish the *Nation* it was Duffy, rather than Dillon or Davis, who proved the more committed entrepreneur in that it was he alone who risked his capital in the new venture. Despite the fact that Duffy, on his first encounter with O'Connell, dismissed him as belonging 'altogether to the nineteenth century', it was in his own Victorian credentials that Duffy clashed most violently with the old man. For it was Duffy, the romantic idealist in politics, who clashed with O'Connell the realist; Duffy the Victorian reformer who collided with O'Connell the Georgian radical; Duffy the prosperous pragmatist in daily affairs who looked askance on O'Connell the ne'er-do-well survivor from an age of credit and endless debt. O'Connell, friend to the abolitionists, abhorred contributions from Irish-American slaveowners; Duffy, the future imperial administrator, was in the camp of those who did not see the point.

The link between journalism and revolution had been established in Ireland (as elsewhere) since the eighteenth century. In 1842 when Duffy began to move his own journalism in such a direction it took him some time to accept that some of the side-effects were squalid rather than romantic. Thus it was that, despite an impassioned 'give me liberty or death' response to an early threat to imprison him, Duffy found it expedient in the last analysis publicly to withdraw the offending remarks. Not surprisingly this incident failed to find a prominent place in Duffy's memoirs. When Duffy's activities finally landed him in a cell in 1848 his first act was to summon his upholsterer 'who fitted up a comfortable bed for him'. Duffy's connection with revolution and its consequences came through his involvement in the Young Ireland movement. Aside from the obvious influence of contemporary European movements of a similar kind, Young Ireland had its beginnings in the steady dissatisfaction of younger members of the Repeal Association with the aged O'Connell and his limited goal of self-government within an imperial framework. The middle-class intellectuals who made up the nucleus of the small movement developed an ideology of separation (or separatism) which in its essence was derived from that of the United Irishmen of the 1790s. More original, however, was their enthusiastic espousal of ancient Irish traditions and their attempts to popularise long-undervalued aspects of Irish history. That their message eventually had racist and sectarian overtones reflected the contemporary state of Irish society as much as the flaws within their theories. *The Nation* was the principal organ through which these theories were propagated. The now familiar irreconcilability between Irish constitutionalism and Irish separatism led to the departure of the Young Ireland element from the Repeal movement. The social desperation brought about by famine conditions and, probably, the influence of parallel insurrections in Europe led the Young Irelanders to attempt a rebellion in 1848. The futility of this ill-planned and disorganised affair was symbolised by the lampooning of its one and only pitched engagement as 'the battle of the Widow McCormick's cabbage-patch'. Recent specialised studies of the Young Irelanders and their personnel have in large part left unaltered the traditional view that they were fine pen-men but hopelessly impractical and ill-prepared revolutionaries. The rising was of course humiliating, and the stigma of 'the Widow McCormick's cabbage-patch' clung to Duffy as it did to those more directly involved. The Young Irelanders' long-term legacy to Irish nationalism lay in the journalistic endeavours which Duffy had done so much to foster. Also, it was through Duffy's writings that Thomas Davis survived in the popular memory to become so significant an ideological lodestone to later nationalists.

By 1849 Duffy had reached another crossroads in his life. Davis was dead, Mitchel, Meagher and O'Brien had been transported, Dillon and D'Ary McGee had fled abroad. Having been faced with the futility of attempting to lead starving and impoverished peasants in revolt, Duffy, a generation before Davitt and Parnell, recognised the importance of material security as a precursor to effective politicisation. It was perhaps due to the experiences of his youth as much as to the influence of Finton Lalor that the extension of the Ulster custom to southern Ireland became the central plank in the platform of the Tenant Rights League. Had matters proceeded less problematically, a long and successful career as an Irish- or London-based constitutionalist may have lain ahead of Duffy. But already he had made the acquaintance of the men whose betrayal would eventually form in his mind the middle-class counterpart to the peasant ineptitude and venality which he had witnessed in 1848. Moreoever, his past as a radical Young Irelander clung disastrously to him in his attempts to woo the essential support of the newly-arrived Cardinal Paul Cullen. The opposition of landed property and Catholic Churchmen to the more important of the League's proposals, together with organisational failures in the countryside and the propensity of the League to become an overtly Dublin-based body, all contributed to Duffy's growing frustration with the Irish scene.

Duffy was, indeed, looking for fresh pastures, but in the event Australia came to him. At the request of members of the Irish communities in Melbourne and Sydney Duffy performed unsuccessfully on their behalf in the matter of the Victorian and New South Wales Constitution Bills, but with a creditable industry for which he was not forgotten. It seems probable that for Duffy journalism had by now reached the limits of whatever satisfaction it could provide. Politically he faced a series of blind alleys. He had been called to the Irish Bar in 1845 but it is likely that any prospects of making a reasonable living at it in Ireland had been hopelessly compromised by his unsteady past and by the opposition of the Catholic Church. It was known, however, that Irish barristers were heading for Victoria in increasing numbers.

Even if Duffy, in a moment of cynicism, had decided to capitalise on his previous experience with the Constitution Bills he could scarcely have foreseen the warmth of the welcome that awaited him in Australia. In brief Duffy found in Australia Irishmen who occupied an environment removed from the conditions created by Irish history. His past in Ireland had given him a pedigree respectable amongst the Irish electorate in

Australia, but the absence of opposing establishment forces meant that he would not have continually to defend, maintain or promote that pedigree. It perhaps understates Duffy's talents and undoubted integrity to suggest that much of his early success in Australia was due to careful exploitation of his laurels and the lack of comparable opposition, but it is at least partly true. Few Irish nationalists ever had the chance to put their theories into practice in an alternative Irish environment, and Duffy made the most of his opportunity. Schemes for a federated Australia which in an Irish context would not have dented the power-structure; land reforms which in Ireland would have been crushed by landlords (and possibly by the clergy also); the consolidation of new political institutions and the building of the new society which in Ireland would have remained a dream — these were the matters which principally occupied Duffy's years in Australian public office. Within a year of becoming a member of the Victoria House of Assembly in 1856, Duffy was appointed Minister of Land but resigned on a point of principle. A period in opposition was followed by a more successful term as Minister for Land and Works during the early 1860s. He was the promoter of anti-squatting legislation which was to prove of some significance to the development of the colony. Following an all-too-brief term as Prime Minister of Victoria in 1871 he was knighted, and then left Australia for several years. On his return in 1876 he was elected Speaker of the House of Assembly, a position he retained until his final retirement from politics in 1880. The embryonic state of development in Australia of some of the institutions which had frustrated him in Ireland was a natural spur to his success. Bigotry of course existed in Australia; but it was less widespread and less pervasive than in his native Ulster. Distance and relative inaccessibility led Westminster to take less interest in the welfare of Australian ranchers than in that of Irish landlords, and so reformers like Duffy found the odds less in their disfavour; in any case Australian land problems were inevitably and essentially of a different hue. Most significantly, Duffy was prepared to conduct his political aspirations securely within an imperial framework; rhetoric apart, his rebel days were over. In the end his departure from Australian politics and from Australia itself was determined by age, overwork, disillusionment and, following the death of his wife in 1878, loneliness. Duffy was married three times in all, the longest in duration being his marriage to Susan Hughes of Newry. His final marriage (in 1881) was to Louise Hall of Cheshire. In all he had ten children, six boys and four girls.

He retired to Nice to write of the past and, occasionally, of the present. Besides his memoirs, his publications included a life of Thomas Davis, a book of conversations with Carlyle, and a history of the Irish Tenant Rights movement of the 1850s. His few literary interventions in the politics of the turbulent 1880s, however, whilst they were received with due interest and respect, had no real impact on events. As in the Australia he had left behind him, Duffy in Ireland had been overtaken by other men and by developments which he could not hope to control or even to influence. His books on the 1840s, re-issued even into the 1960s, remained until very recent years standard works on the events of his time. Their effects on the pre-First World War generation were perhaps incalculable; their effect on the attitudes of post-1922 Irishmen indubitable.

Soon after he had embarked on Australian politics a friend counselled him: 'Never mourn then over "exile" but turn it to the best possible account. That is the part of the true patriot'. To a considerable degree Duffy's positive response to this advice could have made a not inaccurate epitaph to his own life. For he had always been an Ulsterman in exile. Even in death, which overtook him at last in 1903, he lies not in his native Monaghan but in Glasnevin, among the heroes of his young manhood and among later similar figures whose aspirations he would consider himself to have shared. Of his innermost feelings Duffy's writings reveal little, but there is much about his life to indicate that he recognised the universality of the problems which beset Ulster, Ireland and Britain. If this were so, his failure in Ireland and his success in Australia doubtless proved to himself and to others that such problems were not insoluble.

JOHN DUNLAP

c.1746–1812

Printer

Roy McCaughey

JOHN DUNLAP

John Dunlap is regularly celebrated in his native Ulster as the printer of the Declaration of Independence and, in addition, of 'America's oldest daily newspaper'. It is also commonly believed that he learned the printing trade at Gray's, Main Street, Strabane, his home town. Beyond these supposed facts, which are only partially correct, little else is generally known about the man or his career. Not only did Dunlap print the Declaration of Independence: he supported it and fought for it; he acted as official printer to Congress during a crucial period of its existence; he printed the Constitution; and he established America's first successful daily newspaper and in the process made himself extremely wealthy. His importance, therefore, transcends that of merely the printer of one albeit significant document. In fact he holds an honourable position in the history of the printing industry in the United States.[1]

The name 'Dunlap', variations of which include Dunlop, Delap, Dunlevy and Lappin, is of interesting origin and has long associations with the Donegal/Tyrone area.[2] It is, therefore, entirely possible that the Dunlap family of which John was a member lived in the Strabane area for a number of generations, perhaps even before the foundation of Strabane itself. The first definite mention of John Dunlap's family is in a marriage settlement dated 1736 between his father John, a saddler, and James Ector, also a saddler, on behalf of his daughter, Sarah.[3] Neither family had any interest in the printing industry, although Dunlap senior enjoyed a degree of prosperity as mention is made of property owned by him in Strabane. Some clues as to the location of this property are given in an indenture dated 2 February 1780, in which Dunlap senior leased a house on Main Street, Strabane to William Irvine: the property had previously been inhabited by John Gillen.[4] The house was bounded on one side by Robert Finton's freehold (occupied by James O'Donnell, shoemaker) and on the other by Robert Jamison. It was bounded to the rear by the river, a fact which places it firmly on the southern side of Main Street. The property was Dunlap senior's former business address; that it was then rented to another saddler suggests that Dunlap had retired. There is no more precise location for any other property he may have owned, though his will indicates that he did own another property. The will, written in February 1780 and lodged in June 1783, left his saddlery tools to his son Gabriel, his property to his son John, and named William Irvine as one of his executors.[5]

John Dunlap junior was born in 1746 or 1747 and was sent to his uncle William Dunlap in Pennsylvania at approximately the age of ten.[6] He did not therefore, as is popularly believed, learn the printing trade at Gray's of Strabane, nor is there any association between the location of Gray's and his father's saddlery which lay on the opposite side of the street. This is a myth which seems to have been perpetuated by repetition rather than by evidence. The colony to which Dunlap emigrated, in approximately 1757, was one in crisis. The defeat of General Braddock by the French and the Indians in 1755 near modern Pittsburg had thrown the frontier into turmoil: many backcountry settlers fled as refugees to the safer region to the east of the Susquehannah River. The centre of this region was the town of Lancaster where William Dunlap had established a printing business in 1754, having served his apprenticeship under the celebrated printer William Bradford.[7] The town of Lancaster was something of a printing centre for the growing numbers of settlers in the region, to cater for whom Dunlap printed in both English and German. Most of his printing, however, catered for the large numbers of backcountry Presbyterians and their appetite for theological titles. These included four editions of the catechism as authorised by the Assembly of the Church of Scotland; the Rev. Thomas Clark's, *Remarks Upon the*

Manner and Form of Swearing by Touching and Kissing the Gospels (1753); *A Warning of the Presbytery of New Castle, to the People's Care, Against Several Errors and Evil Practices of Mr John Cuthbertson ...* (1754); the Rev. Samuel Delap's, *Remarks on Some Articles of the Seceders' New Covenant And their Act of Presbytery ...* (1754); the Rev. Alexander Gellalty's *A Detection of Injurious Reasonings and Unjust Representations* (1756); and R. Smith's, *Detection Detected, or a Vindication of the Rev'd Mr Delap and New Castle Presbytery* (1757).[8]

In 1757 William Dunlap prudently moved his business from endangered Lancaster to the relative safety of Philadelphia. Whilst in Philadelphia he made yet another wise decision in marrying a relative of Mrs Benjamin Franklin, as a direct result of which he obtained the comfortable position of postmaster. He also re-established his business on Market Street, relying heavily on the sale of books and stationery. In addition he printed works such as *John Jerman's Almanack* (1757) and the annual *Father Abraham's Almanack*, which he inaugurated. John Dunlap, therefore, had a number of considerable advantages at an early age.[9] He was apprenticed to a highly respected and experienced printer, well-connected through business and marriage with the Philadelphia intelligentsia, who also happened to be his childless uncle. Dunlap's success stemmed from his ability to exploit these initial advantages.

By the mid-eighteenth century Philadelphia was not only the largest city in the American colonies (with Lancaster the largest inland town) but also the centre of the colonial printing industry, enjoying particular pre-eminence in type founding.[10] There had also been a paper-making industry in the city since 1690 when William Bradford and William Rittenhouse had established the first plant. The printers realised the importance of these industries and on occasion availed themselves of the profits to be made by investing in them. In 1771 John Dunlap was able to advertise in the *Maryland Gazette* (which he then owned) that he had 'Pennsylvania printing paper of all sorts ...' for sale; while in 1773 he and a number of other Philadelphia printers contributed prize money to encourage the development of a more efficient method of collecting rags for use in the paper industry.[11] John Dunlap's passage to success was further eased by his uncle's decision to enter the ministry. In 1766 William Dunlap, always a keen student of divinity (as his titles suggest), auctioned much of his stock, appointed his nephew as manager of the Market Street printing house as his partner, and travelled to Britain where he was ordained in the Church of England.[12] By the age of twenty, therefore, John Dunlap was in control of one of Philadelphia's premier printing houses — a position enhanced in 1768 when William Dunlap was appointed rector of a parish in Virginia and surrendered his entire interest in the business to his nephew.[13] Thus, instead of having to finish his apprenticeship and either look for employment or try to establish a new printing house, John found his fortune all but made for him by the age of twenty-one. It is possible that his uncle delayed his decision to study for the ministry until such time as Dunlap was old enough to assume responsibility for the printing house: it would appear more than coincidental that the uncle embarked on his clerical career just as his nephew reached a majority. We can also assume that John Dunlap had demonstrated considerable ability for his uncle to display such confidence in him.

Within three years of assuming control Dunlap had switched the emphasis of the business from printing and selling books to printing and selling newspapers. In a period of increasing political tension in the colonies there was a growing demand for news; and, living in a city which was the centre of the printing industry and of the political opposition, it was natural that Dunlap should produce not only a newspaper but one which strongly supported the rights of the colonies. On 21 October 1771 there appeared the first edition of the weekly *Pennsylvania Packet and General Advertiser* (Motto 'whatever men do is the burden of our speech', adopted from Juvenal).[14] In its various forms the paper continued to be printed at the Market Street premises until 1800, apart from the period 1777-78 when Philadelphia was occupied by the British and production moved to Lancaster. In 1775 Dunlap tried to expand his enterprise by establishing a paper in Maryland, *Dunlap's Maryland Gazette; or The Baltimore General Advertiser,* although management of it was quickly entrusted to James Hayes junior, to whom he also sold it in 1778.[15] *The Pennsylvania Packet* had an early competitor in the pro-British *Pennsylvania Chronicle* (published by William Goddard).[16] Dunlap's, and consequently the *Packet's*, pro-American stance ensured the support of the various patriot groups for his newspaper. Indeed, so keen was Dunlap in support of the Colonies' rights that in 1774 he co-founded the First Troop of the Philadelphia City Cavalry.[17] It was Dunlap's early attachment to the revolutionary cause which first drew him to the attention of the Continental Congress: he had published pro-American broadsides after Bunker Hill, Lexington, Ticonderoga and Quebec, and his newspaper was invariably radical in tone. One further practical advantage was that his business on Market Street was quite close to the State House on Chestnut Street.[18] Although Robert Aitken was at this point printer of the *Journals* of the Continental Congress, it was Dunlap whom the revolutionary leaders approached to print the Declaration of Independence and the Articles of Confederation: the task demanded considerable discretion because the documents were at first meant for distribution only to selected individuals and bodies. Perhaps Dunlap was regarded as politically more reliable than Aitken.[19]

A key figure in Dunlap's career was David Chambers Claypoole (1757-1849), who was apprenticed to Dunlap prior to 1771 and showed promise from an early age.[20] He and Dunlap were active in the political agitation which preceded the outbreak of hostilities — Dunlap was a cornet in the City Cavalry and Claypoole a private in an infantry company, and by 1778 he had become Dunlap's junior partner. The role of Claypoole in the preparation, printing and distribution of the Declaration of Independence and the Articles of Confederation should not be underestimated even though he was not yet officially Dunlap's partner. Nor should Dunlap's military activities be overlooked. Despite his business and political affairs, he managed to see active service in the 1776-77 campaign at Princeton and Trenton, a fact borne in mind by the Continental Congress.[21] When Congress temporarily retreated from Philadelphia to Baltimore, Dunlap followed, printing their business on the *Gazette's* presses for which he was rewarded with the largest part of the work.

Following the *Packet's* return from Lancaster in 1778 it appeared as a tri-weekly in competition with the *Pennsylvania Evening Post,* a format followed (with one interruption) until it finally appeared as a daily at the end of the war.[22] Whilst printing the *Packet* Dunlap had also won the contract to print the Congressional *Journals*. However, he lost this contract to his partner Claypoole in 1779.[23] This development appears to have been quite amicable and the *Journals* may even have continued to be printed in the Market Street premises, for in October 1780 Claypoole and Dunlap became full partners in the production of the *Packet*. By the following January Dunlap had relinquished the management of the newspaper to Claypoole and restricted himself to the role of investor.[24] This transfer may have been connected with the libel case between Thomas McKean and General William Thompson, a bitter dispute dating back to 1778 which involved fisticuffs and accusations from Thompson that McKean, the Congressional delegate for Delaware and the Chief Justice of Pennsylvania, had behaved 'like a liar, a rascal, and a coward'. Dunlap printed the allegation in the *Packet,* together with a challenge to a duel, and published McKean's reply. However, McKean sued and in the spring of 1781 was awarded £5,700 damages, part of which was due from the *Packet*. Fortunately, McKean felt vindicated by the decision and released the damages in both cases.[25]

Whether this incident influenced his decision or not, Dunlap temporarily withdrew from public life. He could certainly afford to do so. In 1781 he was able to forward £4,000 for the supply of military provisions.[26] More significantly, he was often paid by Congress not in cash but in land, frequently situated in the city of Philadelphia which was expanding rapidly. Besides a number of city lots Dunlap owned the square between Chestnut and Market Street, and 11th and 12th Streets, and most of the ground on Chestnut Street between 12th and 13th Streets.[27] He subsequently sold the square to Stephen Girard for $120,000.[28] He also purchased 98,000 acres from Virginia (land which after 1792 lay in Kentucky) in Meade and adjoining counties, and he owned the land on which Utica, Indiana, now stands. Dunlap, therefore, not only gained prestige from the Revolution, but also considerable wealth.

In view of his means Dunlap could afford by the age of thirty-five to leave the work in the printing house to Claypoole. By 1784, however, he was back in harness to meet the challenge of turning the *Packet* into a daily, a decision which coincided with Claypoole's dismissal as printer of the *Journals*.[29] The new daily was launched in direct competition with Ben Towne's *Pennsylvania Evening Post*, a daily since 1783. The *Packet*, therefore, was not America's first daily, as is often claimed, but rather its first successful daily. It was an immediate success with a host of distinguished subscribers, including Washington. Dunlap remained active in publishing until his final retirement in 1795: during the intervening period he published a number of titles, always along competitive lines and at one point even in competition with Claypoole. Nor did he restrict himself solely to newspapers: he published the weekly *Die Pennsylvanische Gazette, oder der Allemeine Amerikanische Zeitung-Schreiber*, and the almanac *Der Hoch-Deutch-Americanische Calendar* (1779).[30] In the latter part of his career his most significant publication was the new Constitution in 1787. The Packet even printed the document before the National Congress had passed judgement on it, a clear indication of Dunlap's own opinion of its merits.[31]

Dunlap's military career kept pace with his business life. He served as Lieutenant during the Revolutionary War, was elected Captain in 1794 and became Major in command of the cavalry during the Whiskey Rebellion.[32] On the army's passing through Harrisburg one citizen noted:

> On Friday afternoon, three companies of horse, containing in all, 130, arrived from Philadelphia, the whole under the command of Captain John Dunlap. The company of Light Dragoons, commanded by Captain John Irwin, of this town; the corps of Light Infantry, commanded by Captain George

> Fisher, with the most distinguished officers of the county, were paraded, all in complete uniform, in order to receive them.[33]

During this emergency Dunlap was asked when his unit could be made ready for service. 'When the laws and government of this happy country require defence', he replied, 'the Philadelphia Cavalry need but one hour's notice.'[34]

During the disruption caused by the Revolution Dunlap apparently lost contact with his family in Strabane and did not manage to regain it until 1785. For example, one letter to his sister, Molly Rutherford, was sent to her c/o James Orr of Strabane, Dunlap presumably not having her address.[35] This letter was in response to a request from Orr for Dunlap to sponsor the emigration of his nephew, John Rutherford, 'he being a good clerk and from every information is as good a currier and tanner as left this country'.[36] Dunlap readily agreed to look after his nephew's interests, adding:

> should you think of sending him to this country I will either observe your direction in having him taught some business or judge myself what will be the most suitable for him after he has finished the education you mean to give him — which may be had here as well as in Ireland, for the sooner boys come here after they have determined the better ... I have had six children — two boys and four girls. The boys were both called John and are now with their heavenly Father — the girls are well, viz. Sally, Molly, Nancy and Betsy.[37]

This last information suggests that there had been a considerable break in contact. In a similar letter to his brother-in-law, Robert Rutherford, he noted:

> People with a family advanced in life find great difficulties in emigration, but the young men of Ireland who wish to be free and happy should leave it and come here as quick as possible. There is no place in the world where a man meets so rich a reward for good conduct and industry as in America.[38]

These comments were made in response to rumours that restrictions were to be placed on emigration by the Irish Parliament. Always the astute businessman, Dunlap finshed the letter with a request for 'some little account of the situation of the house in Strabane, whose hands it is in, where the deeds are and what its value may be'. He had, of course, been left the property in his father's will. A near contemporary noted of Dunlap that he 'executed his printing in a neat and correct manner. It is said that, while he conducted a newspaper, he never inserted a paragraph which wounded the feelings of an individual'.[39] This is somewhat difficult to believe of a newspaper owner with strong political convictions, and was certainly not the case in the McKean affair. Having retired permanently from business in 1795, Dunlap sought to live the life of a country gentleman on his estates. This he did, in some splendour, until his death of 'apoplexy' in Philadelphia on 29 November 1812. The funeral in Christ Church cemetery (where Benjamin Franklin is buried) was with full military honours and was a notable event in the city.[40] He left a sumptuous home at 12th and Market Streets, reputedly the finest in the state — so fine in fact that it was subsequently inhabited by Charles Lucien Bonaparte and the ex-King of Spain, Joseph Bonaparte, after their exile.[41] Although he undoubtedly had more than his fair share of advantages, John Dunlap proved himself to be not only an astute businessman but also a strong supporter of the American cause, even when that cause seemed about to fail. When considering Dunlap the printer we should spare a thought for Dunlap the soldier and patriot.

WILLIAM PATERSON

1745–1806

Lawyer and Politician

Steve Ickringill

WILLIAM PATERSON

William Paterson's achievements in public life were considerable and his eventual material success, given his modest origins, would have pleased Horatio Alger or Samuel Smiles. At different times he became Governor of the State of New Jersey, a member of the United States Senate, and a Justice of the United States Supreme Court. He turned down the chance to be Secretary of State and came close to being Chief Justice. At an earlier and decisive stage of his career he was the first Attorney General of revolutionary New Jersey. Just as importantly, he was one of his state's delegates to the Philadelphia Convention of 1787, pursuing a role which continues to excite debate. Throughout his public career he steadily established himself as a man of substance. He became a substantial landowner and a very successful lawyer. He was to die in the home of one of the wealthiest men on the Continent. These public and personal achievements are now well documented, and there has been some telling discussion of his motivation and behaviour. However, there is more to be said, not least because other writers have shown little interest in him as a son of immigrant parents from an Irish Presbyterian background.

Paterson was born in the town of Antrim in 1745. In 1747 the entire family, headed by William's father, Richard (himself born in Scotland), sailed from the port of Londonderry for North America. At a time of sporadic rather than sustained emigration they eventually settled in the village of Princeton, New Jersey, where Richard Paterson became a store-keeper. Here, with a sister and two brothers, William grew up. His father enjoyed modest success for a long time, although eventually he failed in business. Most importantly, the young Paterson watched while Nassau Hall, the largest single building in colonial America at the time, was built between 1754 and 1756. The College of New Jersey (later Princeton University) had found its permanent home and Paterson's life was to be changed decisively as a result. In view of its proximity, attendance at the University was a very practical possibility for the able young man. William graduated B.A. in 1765 and M.A. in 1766. However, at least until his move to Raritan in 1772, Paterson was always in close touch with the College, whether officially a student or not. Among those he came to know were Oliver Elsworth and Luther Martin — just two of the sixteen Princeton graduates who, along with Paterson, were to attend the Federal Convention in Philadelphia in 1787.

Even before his final graduation Paterson had entered the law office of Richard Stockton. Paterson had chosen a prominent lawyer with whom to study. Again edging the story forward, Stockton was one of those who signed the Declaration of Independence. Whatever the future held for Paterson politically, the present was mundane enough in terms of his legal career. He found work hard to come by and his father's bankruptcy was the only boost (if so it may be described) to the frequency of his appearances as a lawyer in court. This happened in 1775, the same year that Paterson was elected to the New Jersey Provincial Congress. His political career, at this stage that of the eager young patriot, was under way.

In the deepening crisis of 1775-6 Paterson proved himself a vigorous and determined Whig. His first major responsibility was as Secretary of the New Jersey Congress. He declined election to the second Congress, but became Secretary after the first session. In 1776 he was selected as a delegate once more and continued to serve as Secretary. After the establishment of the new Constitution for New Jersey and the acceptance of the Declaration of Independence, Paterson was appointed as the first Attorney General of the State of New Jersey. This proved an opportunity to become the hammer of the Tories and to develop an increasingly substantial legal practice. Some idea of the transformation in

Paterson's career can be given with crude statistics. Save for 1775, Paterson never had a double figure of cases before the justices in Hunterdon and Somerset counties. In 1782 he appeared in 124. He appeared as 'Mr. Attorney General' and, on other occasions, as a hard-working lawyer with a rapidly growing practice. His career was a success, just as the Revolution was a success by 1782. During the War (in 1780) his state legislature asked him to serve in the Continental Congress, but he refused. His priority was his work as a private and public lawyer. He knew well enough the costs and complications of serving in Congress.

Paterson retired as Attorney General in 1783. He flourished in the succeeding years of peace. He suffered no 'Critical Period'. Among his new clients was James Parker, best described as a 'Tory-neutral' during the War. Quaker merchants from Philadelphia of similar pasts also joined his list of clients. Elias Boudinot, a fellow Jerseyman and sometime President of the Continental Congress, was helpful in introducing Paterson to other prosperous clients. Whatever their political records the rich and influential found Paterson worth his hire. He himself became not only a good lawyer, but a well-connected one. Now ambitious young men wanted to study in his office — rather than Richard Stockton's! The former Attorney General enjoyed his three hundred acre estate on the Raritan river. This estate had been owned by a prominent member of the colonial Bar who had stayed loyal to the Crown and fled New Jersey. The estate's confiscation had enabled Paterson to make an impressive purchase. Lagrange, the lawyer who had previously owned the land, was not the only colonial lawyer to become an emigré. It was Cortland Skinner's decision to flee the colony that had left the position of Attorney General open. In a number of ways Paterson had made the most of his opportunities.

The story so far can make Paterson seem a man cynically on the make, and there is no doubt of his hunger for success and financial security. Nonetheless some obvious points need emphasis. Paterson chose the revolutionary cause, though it could have cost him his life. His devotion to the cause was as great as his pursuit of his own personal advancement. He was the product of Whiggish, Presbyterian Princeton. John Witherspoon, the most influential of that College's eighteenth-century Presidents, was (as John Adams said) 'an animated Son of Liberty'. We would probably want to add that Paterson's immigrant background inevitably made him suspicious of the British Crown, and jealous of his rights and those of his fellow Americans. What is striking is the way in which this undoubted and dangerous commitment went hand in hand with personal advancement. Paterson was clear on the matter:

> It is a leading and well grounded Principle with Politicians that those who are in Power should always so rule as to make it the Interest of the People to Side with Government. For it is a truth which holds equally good in political and private life, that Interest is the Pole Star by which the Map of Mankind steer their course.

John Adams would have heartily concurred.

Paterson was persuaded back into public life in 1787. He joined William Livingston, David Bearly, Jonathon Dayton and, briefly, W. C. Houston as the New Jersey delegates to the Federal Convention in Philadelphia. In the early weeks of the Convention Paterson proved himself a stubborn and effective debater. This time the interest he was defending was that of his state and, to some extent, of similar states within the Union. He maintained the 'small state' position with the forensic skill to be expected of a successful lawyer. Paterson was anything but what would be later called a states righter, still less a 'proto' anti-federalist. He accepted the need for a stronger form of central government, while wanting to see his own state's influence, and even its power, maintained.

The initiative in the Convention was taken by the Virginian delegation. They received significant support for their 'nationalist' plan, notably from the Pennsylvanian and Massachusetts delegations. The support for the position of one large state from two other large states was particularly notable to William Paterson. To him and others the Virginian plan was a 'large-state' plan. Paterson took the initiative in rallying small states against it. On Saturday 9

June Paterson rose to make one of his major speeches:

> We have no power to go beyond the federal scheme and if we had the people are not ripe for any other. We must follow the people, the people will not follow us ... A confederacy supposes sovereignty in the members comprising it and sovereignty supposes equality. If we are to be considered as a nation all State distinctions must be abolished, the whole must be thrown into hotchpot, and when an equal division is made, then there may be fairly an equality of representation.

He went on to emphasise that there was a need for a strong central government, but not a government based on a system of representation proportional to population.

It can be imagined how sections of this speech, as reported by Madison, have led scholars into speculation. It has been suggested that Paterson was a thoroughgoing democrat and/or thoroughly committed to states' rights. Ironically it is with the unlikely reference to 'hotchpot' that the key to Paterson's real position lies — a reference easily dismissed as an awkward debating point. Certainly the observation is a clear expression of suspicion at what Paterson and his colleague, Brearly, saw as large state nationalism. For them large state nationalism was indistinguishable from large state aggrandisement. Later in the Convention a genuinely angry Paterson observed that he had been told that his talk of hotchpot was impractical: 'Let it be tried, and we shall see whether the citizens of Massachussets, Pennsylvania and Virginia accede to it.' This was arguably a response to a similarly belligerent remark by James Wilson, made as early as 5 June, when he said that any ratification of the new constitution should be so organised as to allow partial union, with a door ajar to allow others to enter eventually. Madison himself noted that this remark was meant *in terrorem* to the smaller states.

There was more going on, however, than threat and counter threat. From one of the drafts of the Small State plan drawn up to counter the Virginia plan, (the Small State plan is also known as the New Jersey or Paterson plan) it becomes clear that a fundamental aspect of the discussion was the question of the western lands. New Jersey was a 'landless state', like, say, Maryland and Delaware: that is, New Jersey had no claims to western land. Virginia, by extreme contrast, had positively continental claims. Paterson's argument, reflecting his own state's long-established position, was that all such lands were the common property of the United States, who were sovereign over them as the King had once been. It also has to be said that there were many western land speculators in New Jersey, and that land speculation was close to the heart of Luther Martin from Maryland, one of Paterson's old Princeton friends and an ally in the creation of the Paterson plan.

It was another Princeton graduate and contemporary, Oliver Ellsworth (also born in 1745), who was one of the key figures in engineering the compromise in representation which resulted in the fundamental difference in the principle of representation between the United States Senate and the House of Representatives. Paterson served on the committee which proposed the 'Great Compromise', but he viewed it as second best to his own plan. For Paterson, the people did not complain of the old system as such; rather they wanted a Congress with more power. Power was the central issue. Paterson wanted a more powerful government, not least to deal with western lands, but he wanted his state to have the maximum possible say in the use of that power. After the 'Great Compromise' had been accepted Paterson behaved characteristically: he went home to get on with his private affairs, returning only to sign the new Constitution. He had achieved all he could for his state and was now happy to see the creation of a stronger central government.

Before continuing with Paterson's personal story — in rather less detail! — one more element in his thinking needs to be emphasised. This is in one way re-emphasis, as it takes us back to states and land, and related perceptions. There is a morose note in one of Paterson's own speech summaries as he listens to James

Wilson asking what the small states think they have to fear at the hands of the large states. What examples are there, demands the Pennsylvanian (and graduate of the University of Edinburgh), of large states partitioning smaller neighbours. 'Poland' is Paterson's brief entry. With the benefit of hindsight this might seem overstated, but it was real enough. Above all, Virginia, bloated in size and unwilling to relinquish land claims, was a threatening presence to Paterson and other small state delegates. With the Connecticut compromise which Ellsworth did so much to engineer, Paterson's worst worries could be held at bay. Given the taxing power of the new government, New Jersey would no longer be in thrall to the duties charged by New York and Pennsylvania on either side of her. Paterson could watch with some complacency as New Jersey's ratifying Convention overwhelmingly accepted the new form of government.

In 1788 Paterson was elected, very appropriately, to serve in the Senate of the United States. He proved himself a loyal supporter of Washington's first administration. In particular he was staunch in his support of Alexander Hamilton's financial measures. He was entirely convinced of the need to honour the national debt at face value. Contracts were sanctified. Indeed, Paterson was more determined on this issue than Hamilton himself. Paterson had seen threats to the sanctity of contract in New Jersey in the 1780s, when legislation had attempted to make life easier for debtors. As a lawyer he was clear on the matter and, as a staunch defender of property rights, even clearer. To give Paterson his due, when his own brothers and brother-in-law disappeared leaving Paterson with a great deal of expensive paper, he struggled to honour these obligations while writing some very bitter letters.

Paterson's career in the Senate was short as in 1791 he was elected as the second Governor of the State of New Jersey. It was a signal honour to succeed William Livingston, a member of one of the great 'Patroon' families of neighbouring New York. There was no question of a contested election in the New Jersey assembly. Paterson gained unanimous support. As with many other state constitutions at the time, the role of Governor was limited in New Jersey, but the office was one of great dignity, and the ease with which Paterson gained the position emphasises the widespread confidence in him among politically active Jerseymen. He had become the first citizen of a state he had served well. As Governor, Paterson is chiefly remembered for two things. He was asked to begin a major reform, revision and codification of the state's legal code and, indeed, the court practice of his state. This massive task was to occupy him long after he ceased to be Governor, but he managed to complete it by 1799. Secondly, and even more significantly for posterity, he signed the Charter which created the Society for Establishing Useful Manufactures. The Society named their site of operations, Paterson, New Jersey.

Governor Paterson was involved in the Society from its establishment in 1791. His family did have a direct interest in the financial success of the project, although William's own involvement was not large. Certainly, he faced financial problems because of his brothers' debts, which gave rise to obligations which he had to discharge. Perhaps it would be fair to say that his involvement in the project re-emphasises much of what we have already discovered about Paterson. He was self-interested, but he also thought that the Society would be of real benefit to his state, and to the United States. Further, it is not surprising to discover that other prominent Americans were among the project's promoters. Perhaps most notably, Alexander Hamilton, the Secretary to the United States Treasury, personally prepared the document which went before the New Jersey Assembly when the Society was petitioning for its corporate charter and special privileges. Sadly, the Jerseymen and New Yorkers who were involved saw little benefit for themselves in the short term. With William Duer at its head the Society soon became a very speculative venture, as Paterson himself recognised. Indeed, during Paterson's life-time, the town of Paterson constituted an embarrassment — a ghost town. L'Enfant, the architect of Washington D.C., was also involved in the design of Paterson; and he was never a lucky man. Long after Paterson's death, and indeed L'Enfant's demise in penury, the town became duly incorporated and for a time at least in the nineteenth century was a major industrial centre.

In 1793 Paterson made the last major move of his public career when he accepted appointment as a Justice of the United States Supreme Court. He was to be a member of the Court until his death. As indicated earlier, this was not because he lacked other offers of high office. In 1795 he turned down the chance to be Secretary of State: acceptance at this juncture, during the crisis over Jay's Treaty, was a worrisome prospect and Paterson was not the only one to refuse Washington's offer of the job, although he was the first to do so. It must be recognised that Paterson was acutely aware of his own ignorance of foreign affairs, which makes his unwillingness to serve doubly understandable. It also reminds us of how much confidence Washington had in him. However, Paterson found the Supreme Court thoroughly congenial. He could combine his personal, legal and business career with the important office of a Supreme Court Justice. He certainly did not decline to serve in Washington's Cabinet out of any lack of loyalty to the President, or to the Federalist Party which, in reluctant practice, Washington now led. As a Supreme Court Justice Paterson proved himself a fervent supporter of the Federalist cause. He could properly be described as a politicised judge in the 1790s, and he was happy to remain so.

The Crisis of 1798 clearly demonstrated how partisan Paterson could be. In that year in the almost frantic atmosphere brought on by international crisis and vigorous internal party conflict, the Federalists pushed through the Alien and Sedition Acts. These measures restricted both immigration and the right of free speech. As an immigrant and son of immigrants Paterson might have been expected to be more sympathetic to the rights of newcomers, but in the context of a world made dangerous by revolutionary France he showed no such sympathy. Paterson positively relished the opportunity to preside in the case of Mathew Lyon, prosecuted under the Sedition Act. Lyon, himself from an Irish background, was in the view of Judge Paterson guilty of uttering sedition, and he made his view quite clear to the jury. Paterson sent Lyon to jail for four months and fined him $1,000. Paterson was a political judge, whether we look at his performance in 1798 or at the time of the 'Whiskey Rebellion' in 1795. When he saw the republic threatened or the rights of property challenged (the two were synonymous in his mind) he was relentless. As when in the United States Senate he was even more determined than Hamilton on the issue of the National Debt, he proved himself a Federalist among Federalists as a Judge in the years before 1801.

Paterson's remaining years on the bench were less controversial. It seemed possible in 1801 that he might become Chief Justice, but in his notorious 'midnight appointments' President John Adams preferred John Marshall. It is also worth saying that Paterson himself did not actively seek the position; rather that committed Federalists saw in him an excellent check to the incoming administration of Thomas Jefferson. Very importantly, once Jefferson had triumphed and the 'Revolution of 1800' was complete, Paterson showed markedly less hysteria than some of his fellow Federalists. He grasped that something less than atheistical Jacobinism was to be unleashed in America. Ultimately Paterson became convinced that Jefferson was, like himself, a supporter of the Constitution and the republican institutions that went with it.

More personally, Paterson's remaining years were very satisfying. He continued to prosper as a lawyer and property owner. Just as the New Jersey Assembly had honoured him with election to Governor, and Washington by offering the key Cabinet post, his alma mater did likewise by making him a Trustee of the College of New Jersey. Later Harvard University gave him an honorary degree, quite properly that of Doctor of Laws. His own son graduated from Princeton and followed his father into the legal profession, albeit in New York City rather than in New Jersey. If such personal success for himself and career choice by his son gave pleasure, his daughter's fate must have delighted him. In 1802 Cornelia Paterson married Stephen Van Renselaer, the greatest of the Patroons of the Hudson Valley in New York State. Cornelia, much his junior, was Van Renselaer's second wife and a more impressive match would not have been possible in America at that time. Van Renselaer was active in politics but more importantly he was the owner of tens of thousands of acres and landlord to large numbers of tenant farmers. Paterson might reasonably have thought that the granddaughter of an Irish immigrant storekeeper had done rather well. In September 1806 Paterson died at the Van Renselaer manor house in Albany. His own journey from the emigrant ship had been a remarkable one.

No great mention has been made of Paterson's ethnicity and religion: this omission prompts one major point about Paterson. As a Presbyterian and an Irish or Scotch-Irish immigrant, he successfully disappeared into the dominant American culture. In his adopted state of New Jersey Paterson's success ensured his acceptance, as it did in the broader context of the United States as a whole. Through his daughter's marriage Paterson joined the social elite even more clearly than he had done previously. This view does not contradict the earlier point about Paterson's strong commitment to the Revolution. Many of the old colonial elite took a prominent role in the Revolution, not least the Livingstons and Van Renselaers. Now, in this context Paterson's experience was obviously untypical of the great majority of Scotch-Irish immigrants and their descendants in colonial, revolutionary and early national America. Of course there were individuals such as Dunlap, Thomson and McHenry whose careers were to some extent similar to Paterson's, but they were in a small minority. For the most part the immigrants stayed in modest circumstances while taking an active part in the Revolution and subsequently in radical politics. The greatest concentration of these first Irish Americans was in Pennsylvania, where they enjoyed a turbulent, sometimes dominant role in state politics. Like Paterson in New Jersey in the early revolutionary years, they were good Whigs, but unlike him they remained in the forefront of radical politics. They supported the Pennsylvania Constitution with its unicameral system, they were the bedrock of anti-Federalism, and they were at the heart of the Jeffersonian party in the keystone state. The link between Irish Americans and, to William Paterson, the hated Democratic Party is a long one.

Significantly, however untypical Paterson and a few other distinguished Irish immigrant contemporaries may have been, their experience presaged that of many of those with an Irish Presbyterian heritage in the future. As has often been emphasised, in the long term the Scotch Irish ceased to be visible as a recognisable group in the United States, although there were significant exceptions. Accepting the overall force of the generalisation, however, the comparison with Paterson's personal experience is instructive. Like Paterson the Scotch-Irish found it relatively easy in the long term to join the mainstream, if not the elite, of white Anglo-Saxon Protestant America. Its values were their values. Paterson was no staunch Presbyterian, to the disappointment of that church's clergy in New Jersey. He espoused Christian values, even championed them, but not in a vigorously sectarian way. The hold of the Presbyterian Church was to prove similarly weak on many immigrants who shared Paterson's origins. Paterson was an early example of how an immigrant could fully, even dramatically, join not just the mainstream but the dominant group in society. Over the subsequent decades this was to be the pattern for the Scotch-Irish, though few of them were to achieve a burial ground comparable to the Van Renselaer family plot.

JOHN ABERNETHY

1680–1740

Scholar and Ecclesiast

A. Godfrey Brown

JOHN ABERNETHY

Presbyterianism in Ireland in the early eighteenth century found itself embroiled in at least two major controversies. One was an internal conflict over religious liberty, particularly in matters of doctrine, focusing upon the obligation to subscribe to the Westminster Confession of Faith. The other was a controversy over religious liberty and the rights and freedoms of the citizen, focusing upon the Test Acts. One of the major figures in both debates was a distinguished minister, first in Antrim, and then in Dublin, the Reverend John Abernethy. The purpose of this essay is to give some account of his life and writings, and in particular to analyse what we can discover about his contribution to these two major features of Presbyterian history.

John Abernethy was born on 19 October 1680. The Abernethys were a Scottish clan and the first member of the immediate family to settle in Ireland was the Rev. John Abernethy, the father of our subject, who became Minister of Brigh, Co. Tyrone, in 1680. Four years later he removed to Moneymore where he and his family were living when the Revolution overtook Ireland. Abernethy, together with the Rev. Patrick Adair, the historian, had been appointed by a meeting of Presbyterian ministers, held at Connor on 22 January 1689, to go to England in order to present an address of congratulation to William, Prince of Orange, and express the loyalty of the Ulster Presbyterians to him and to his cause. During his absence severe civil disorder broke out. John himself had been sent to board with relatives in Ballymena, and in the panic and confusion of the times was taken by them across to Scotland, having 'no opportunity of conveying him to his mother ...' She had fled to Londonderry, and in the ensuing siege of Derry lost all her other children. Master John continued his education in Scotland for almost three years, staying with his maternal grandmother — the family of Walkingshaw, Renfrewshire — until rejoining his parents in Coleraine, where his father had become Minister in November 1691.

John Abernethy's academic career was a remarkable one. At thirteen he became a student at Glasgow University where he duly obtained his M.A. His intention was to go on to study medicine, but he yielded to the persuasions of parents and friends and decided to study for the ministry. He took his theological course at Edinburgh under Professor George Campbell, a sound scholar in a solidly Calvinist tradition. The period 1690-1703 saw a considerable number of Irish Presbyterian theological students attending Edinburgh, and included in that number were some of the ablest men of their day, of whom Abernethy was certainly one. It was written of him:

> His distinction at Glasgow college and his social attainments preceded him. He was at once admitted into the innermost circle of the cultured society of Edinburgh. The unvarying tradition is that he excelled as a conversationalist, drawing forth the wonder of grave professors (e.g. of Professor Campbell) and the more perilous homage of fair ladies' bright eyes.[1]

When his formal studies in Edinburgh were complete John Abernethy returned to Coleraine to undertake the usual period of private study. He was licensed by the Presbytery of Route on 3 March 1702, but since he was still under twenty-one he went to Dublin to engage in further formal reading and study. At that time Thomas Emlyn was colleague to Joseph Boyse in the influential Wood Street congregation and, having been found guilty of holding an Arian view of the person of Christ, he was brought before the courts and in due course imprisoned for blasphemy. Abernethy, having preached in Wood Street, was invited to succeed Emlyn. He was also in receipt of calls from Antrim, and from Coleraine as successor to his father. He decided to come north, and accepted the ruling of the General Synod of Ulster that he go to Antrim. He was duly ordained and installed there on 18

August 1703. He married an Antrim lady, Susannah Jordan. She died in 1712 leaving him with one son and three daughters.

His ministry in Antrim lasted for twenty-seven years and was by all accounts energetic and successful. His early years were marked by a notable piety and evangelistic zeal, particularly towards the native Irish speakers who lived on the shores of Lough Neagh.[2] It appears he was successful to a considerable degree in converting a number of them from Catholicism to the Reformed faith.[3] Above all his ministry was marked by a high degree of scholarship, and Duchal, his successor and biographer, has pointed out that he knew a great deal, not only of books but of public affairs too.[4] His preaching was marked by a freshness of thought that made him most attractive to his hearers. His voice was clear and strong, but his real talent lay in forceful argument and well-reasoned convictions. This was to become increasingly obvious with the years. His early preaching, however, had both tenderness and enthusiasm which more than compensated for being sometimes over the heads of his hearers.[5]

Two sermons survive from this early period of his ministry. The first was preached at Antrim to mark the accession of George I.[6] It was a defence of popular consent as a basis for monarchy against the Stuart theory of Divine Right. Its basic content, so similar to many Presbyterian sermons on the national occasions of that period, extolled public righteousness and warned of retribution against the nation that forsook the ways of God. It bewailed the vice of the time and called upon the Royal Family to set a godly example. The sermon was well-phrased and yet lacked the 'fire' of many similar contemporary efforts. The other example of Abernethy's early preaching was a curious sermon commending the study of Scripture prophecy as a duty Christians owe to what God has revealed in scripture, and as a strength to faith and an expression of earnest desire for the Church's glorious consummation. Abernethy held that the end was almost certainly just at hand and went so far as to agree in a tentative way with current computations of 1716 as the probable date. The sermon is of interest both because it reveals strong anti-Roman Catholic convictions, sentiments shared by almost all, even of the most liberal Protestant divines, and also because Abernethy expressed his belief that the fundamental doctrine of Christ's deity was plainly evidenced by scripture. Thus:

> In like manner, though we have not such perfect overbearing proof, for some matters contained in the revelation: such as the time of Antichrist's fall, and the commencement of the millenium, as we have for the essential doctrines of faith, the deity of our Saviour, and the redemption of the elect by his death; yet we ought to believe, resting in such evidence, as the wisdom of God has been pleased to give us.[7]

It was the publication of Abernethy's third work, however, that brought his name before the public and indeed marked the beginning of the subscription controversy. Behind the sermon lay a personal dissatisfaction on Abernethy's part with the conduct of the General Synod of Ulster, part of whose function was to supervise the call of ministers to congregations within their bounds, especially in cases of conflict. It was Synod, as we have seen, that decided in favour of Abernethy's going to Antrim in 1703, and at that time he had expressed himself willing to submit to its decision.[8] In 1712 he had received a call to Londonderry, but had been overjoyed when Synod had decided to keep him in Antrim.[9]. In 1717-18 Abernethy had again to face the dilemma of a call away from Antrim, this time from the congregation of Usher's Quay in Dublin and, at almost the same time, another from the Old Congregation of Belfast. This time Synod resisted the pleas of Abernethy and the Antrim congregation, and ruled in favour of Dublin.[10] Very reluctantly he went to Dublin for three months, but decided it was not for him, and in defiance of Synod returned to Antrim and renewed his ministry there. A year later Abernethy was still in Antrim, and put forward earnest pleas to resist removal to Dublin. This time Synod, which had transferred him to the Presbytery of Dublin, told him to go on trial for at least eight months, and then if he still felt unable to see this as the will of God, to negotiate with the Dublin Presbytery to release him.[11] In the event Abernethy did not go to Dublin, but corresponded with the Presbytery of Dublin who eventually bowed to the inevitable, and agreed to release him from his call to Usher's Quay, and to allow him to resettle in the North. Synod itself in 1720 accepted the situation, though giving it as their opinion 'that Mr Abernethy ought to have gone to Dublin, according to appointment, and was faulty in not doing so,'.[12] The whole experience had been a bitter one for Abernethy, and had confirmed him in views which were gaining increasing acceptance amongst a circle of his friends and colleagues, questioning the authority of Church courts over the liberty of individual conscience, and not least the imposition of credal tests such as subscription to the Westminster Confession of Faith.

The group of people amongst whom these views were gaining momentum in the north of Ireland found their focus in an organisation known as the Belfast Society. The closing years of the seventeenth century and the early years of the eighteenth century saw the flowering of religious societies of many kinds, and not least the existence of student societies in the Scottish universities, where so many ministers of the Synod of Ulster received their education. The Belfast Society was formed around the year 1705, and was made up of ministers and students for the purposes of prayer and discussion. Ministerial poverty made the expense of an extensive library out of the question for most ministers, and the first members were anxious to pool their resources so that they could buy different books, except where constant use demanded individual ownership, and share with one another the fruits of their reading. It was a practice by no means unique in that day, or indeed since! The membership of the Society at first comprised men drawn from different presbyteries, but convenience of residence was really a decisive factor. An early attempt was made to diversify, and set up societies in different presbyteries to meet after presbytery meetings, and so include all members of presbytery in the discussions. While this admirable ideal met with some favour, it was soon rendered impracticable by the pressure of presbytery business and the lengthy journeys that faced many of the members. In the end it was decided to revert to the original plan of meeting centrally in Belfast.[13]

The content of the discussions ranged over the whole subject of doctrine and pastoral practice, and the interpretation of controverted passages of scripture. A fascinating account of the meetings of the Society has been compiled by Kirkpatrick in the conclusion to Duchal's *Sermon on the Death of Abernethy*.[14] He records that sermons were preached before the Society upon such titles as the nature and scriptural terms of Christian unity, schism, the rights of conscience, and of private judgement, the sole dominion of Christ in His own kingdom, excommunication and other subjects. At each meeting two members were appointed to prepare a detailed study of several chapters of scripture, one from the Old Testament and one from the New Testament. At the next meeting they were to interpret these in the light of the best commentaries available, dealing especially with controverted passages. This would lead to discussion, and on occasion to special study at a subsequent meeting of some of the problems raised. It was open to any member to raise any special problem or question that he happened to have in mind. Without fettering this right, the Society hoped to proceed in an orderly fashion to cover eventually the whole of scripture.

Part of every meeting was devoted to 'A Communication of Studies' in which members shared the fruits of their own private reading, and encouraged the disposition to regular study. The main business, however, was a lengthy paper upon a set subject chosen by the members. Their principle was stated thus:

> We have endeavour'd to chuse such subjects of divinity as we judg'd most profitable; and which seem'd to have the greatest influence upon practical religion: For we consider the gospel as a doctrine according to godliness; carefully avoiding over-curious and unscriptural speculations; endeavour to learn the truth as it is in Jesus, and to distinguish it from questions & strifes about Words, ...[15]

Among the subjects chosen were the existence of God, and the natural and moral perfections of the Deity, the foundations of natural religion and of morality, the truth and excellence of Christianity, the native tendency of Christianity to restore human nature to its true dignity, to give a true understanding of God and inspire love for Him and to direct to an elevated and rational piety. They also considered the evidences for Christianity such as miracles, prophecy, the resurrection of Jesus, the gifts of the Holy Ghost, and the rapid progress of the gospel. The principal objections raised against the Christian faith by unbelievers were also studied.

Members of the society evidenced a great concern about Protestant disunity and devoted time to consider the best characteristics of Lutherans and Calvinists, the Episcopal, Presbyterian and Congregational forms, as well as early Continental Protestant movements such as the Vaudois. This ecumenical study they held to be consistent with the liberty of dissenters to use the best customs and practices of any age of the Church.[16] They were also concerned about the improvement of their own pastoral efficiency and discussed preaching, sick visitation, how to strengthen the weak, reprove the wicked and admonish good folk who had fallen into a fault.[17]

All this was clearly good and valuable, and the members spoke warmly of the benefits that they gained from their mutual fellowship. The problem, however, was that the Society became identified with one particular emphasis or cause, namely that of liberty, and, bedevilled by the indiscretions of some of its own members, and by the inherent dangers in its chief doctrine, it soon gave rise to suspicion and rumour that culminated in the bitter subscription controversy that lasted for seven years and tore the Synod asunder.

It was the publication of a sermon of Abernethy's, preached before the Belfast Society on 19 December 1719 and entitled *Religious Obedience founded on Personal Persuasion*,[18] that created the fear amongst many orthodox ministers of the Synod that the disturbing views already evident across the Irish Sea and in the Emlyn case in Dublin were now manifesting themselves in the Synod itself. The sermon held that authority in matters religious is not to be based upon the judgment of others, or even of Church Courts, but upon the personal persuasion of the individual conscience after the most deliberate and unprejudiced quest after the truth. Abernethy based his sermon upon Rom. xiv, 5, and while he admitted that the context of Paul's words was concerned with a matter of indifference and not the great central affirmations of the gospel, he went on to imply that the same principle must hold even in these vital matters;[19] and that even in exercising this right of private judgment, Church courts were not to constrain a man's convictions. The Church's power was only for edification, not for imposition.[20] Right through the sermon Abernethy seemed to hint that there was a residuum of doctrine that must be regarded as essential, and yet he nowhere attempted to define it. Indeed in the final paragraph he flung the door wide open:

> ...it is so evident that our Lord Jesus Christ has not only granted all his disciples the privilege, but strictly enjoin'd them to enquire into his will revealed in the gospel, that from thence they may learn what to believe, and what to practise, and without submitting implicitly to human declarations and decisions in any point of faith or duty, may by following impartially their own light, the full persuasion of their own minds, obtain his approbation.[21]

Thus Abernethy's plea for liberty that so elegantly expressed the whole ethos of the Belfast Society opened the door to the greatest possible laxity about doctrine even of the most essential kind.

Abernethy was not at heart a controversialist, and it was in a sincere attempt to mollify the fears of the orthodox that he published anonymously in 1722 his *Seasonable Advice to the Protestant Dissenters*.[22] This tract was directed in particular to the laity of the Church which had been greatly upset by the mounting rumour of heterodoxy. Lay pressure had forced a good many ministers to make a voluntary subscription, and this had had the effect of isolating even more those whose principles made it impossible for them to subscribe. Abernethy admitted that not all non-subscribers had spoken or acted wisely:

> I know it will be said that some Ministers gave too great occasion for suspecting them as inclined to opinions which are generally reputed new, and of a dangerous tendency; and in particular, that they expressed less regard than others had, or themselves once seemed to have, for the Westminster Confession, or at least for some uses which are commonly made of it among the Northern Presbyterians.[23]

Yet, he held, non-subscription of itself was no proof of error, and the Synod had declared itself satisfied as to the orthodoxy of all its ministers, and the non-subscribers themselves had given every assurance of their orthodoxy short of subscribing man-made statements of faith. Hence, he argued, to exclude them from ministerial communion would be an act of schism on the part of subscribers,[24] and for the laity to forsake a minister for his non-subscribing principles would be to deny Presbyterianism for a corrupt form of Independency.[25]

Abernethy's argument lacked conviction, however, to this extent, that he offered no solid factual evidence of his own or his brethren's real doctrinal position. The principle of liberty was all important. The issue of doctrinal purity seemed largely a matter of indifference. This studied ambiguity on matters doctrinal is evidenced even more plainly in the lengthy *Defence of the Seasonable Advice* which Abernethy published under his own name in 1724 in reply to Mastertown's *Apology*, an attack on his earlier work. In it he expanded his earlier line of argument, answering in considerable detail every point his opponent had made. In particular he defended the non-subscriber's action in refusing to submit to any imposed form of words as an authoritative test of orthodoxy, and declared that the only scriptural way to deal with error was to make charges and show proofs. To require men to purge themselves of heterodoxy, or any other offence, by giving their own testimony against unspecified suspicions is contrary, he held, both to Christian discipline and common equity.[26] Abernethy again cited the fact that those present at the 1721 Synod had expressed themselves satisfied with the orthodoxy of the non-subscribers on Christ's Deity.[27] It was on the principle of liberty alone that they took their stand:

> Because the Synod's Declaration concerning the independent deity of our Saviour had so great appearance of contrariety [sic] to this principle, that was one reason why we judg'd it in those circumstances unseasonable, however both true and important the doctrine itself still was acknowledged to be;[28]

As for the charge that they held the truth of this doctrine, but not its importance, Abernethy wrote:

> that tho' the importance of the doctrine was very evident to themselves, in their view of the Christian scheme, yet they cou'd not take upon them to pronounce damnation (which is the strict and proper sense of declaring fundamentality) on men for not believing any principle, or explication of a principle, unless God himself has done it by some plain Scripture declaration: Upon this it appear'd that there was no difference between the Non-Subscribers and other members of the Synod, in this particular.[29]

Yet, however much Abernethy asserted that refusal to subscribe was not due to disagreement with the doctrine of the Westminster Confession, he failed to speak in the strong and reassuring terms that might have disarmed his opponent's fears. His arguments offered no real security against the inroads of error, and indeed his statements were at points so unguarded that his subscribing brethren might well have been left wondering if he and his friends regarded any doctrine as absolutely fundamental except perhaps the existence of God. Thus he wrote:

> ...the great rule of righteousness to do as we would be done by, requires us to extend our charity to those who have failures, knowing that we ourselves are compassed with infirmity; and methinks errors in judgment which do

> not affect the vitals of religion, have in some respects a better claim to charitable forbearance than faults in practice.[30]

Nowhere, however, in the *Defence* did Abernethy define what were the vitals of religion! In his *Sermon* preached at Antrim in the same year Abernethy again drew the distinction between matters of greater and lesser importance in theology, but again failed to elaborate. He held that no detail of truth was too trivial but that a man should adhere to it and never give it up, yet at the same time where it was a matter of little consequence he should exercise a charitable forbearance towards those who differed from him.

> I think it will be very evident to any one who attentively considers the strain of the sacred writings, that there are some doctrines and precepts of Christianity which are of its very essence, and wherein, therefore, all Christians must be agreed; and some things more doubtful and of lesser importance, wherein the sincere may differ...[31]

Yet for all the tantalising absence of definition, Abernethy asserted in this sermon also that none of the non-subscribers had been charged 'with Principles which have ever been esteem'd Heretical (as far as I know) by the Primitive or Reform'd Churches.'[32]

In his *Letter to Mr John Malcome*, published in 1726, Abernethy had to make answer to precisely such a charge, though it was evidently based upon rumour, and not upon fact.

> Your next proof is, that one of the Belfast Society told a subscriber that we are all agreed that the common scheme of the Trinity cannot be defended; but what scheme to fall on we are not yet agreed. To my certain knowledge, the story is utterly false, but who is the author of it I hope will soon appear, if you are so just as to discover your information.[33]

Abernethy was quick to point out that the greatest defenders of the doctrine of the Trinity — Calamy, Boyse, Wats, Oldfield and Hughes — had been non-subscribers.[34]

After the exclusion of the non-subscribers Abernethy did not remain long in the North. Witherow conjectures a three-fold cause for his departure from Antrim:

> Cut off from the public field on which he had so often exercised his controversial powers, finding no excitement in the society of a handful of men holding opinions similar to his own, and mortified by the withdrawl of a large portion of his own people, who formed themselves into a new congregation in connexion with the Synod, Abernethy felt so uncomfortable in Antrim as to be ripe for removal any day.[35]

The real reason, however, was the call to succeed the late Joseph Boyse in Wood Street, Dublin. It was an important charge, and Boyse had undoubtedly been the brightest star in the Irish Presbyterian firmament. Whether or not the move indicated any feeling of frustration with the narrow confines of the Presbytery of Antrim we cannot say.

The principles of liberty, however, remained dear to Abernethy, and he defended them as we shall see on a new battle-ground, a pamphlet on *The Nature and Consequences of the Sacramental Test considered*,[36] and a series of pamphlets entitled *Reasons for the Repeal of the Sacramental Test*.[37] The argument was in the main political, and no substantial evidence of Abernethy's theology really emerges from them. One point, however, is worthy of note. Abernethy's orthodoxy on the deity of Christ may, I think, be deduced from the following:

> The divine author of our religion, to perpetuate the memory of his death for our redemption, appointed the Holy Sacrament in commemoration of it, to be a badge of the Christian profession, and that his followers might by that religious solemnity declare their faith in him, and their purposes of a sincere and constant obedience to his laws.[38]

Yet the emphasis is surely neo-nomian. The gospel is a new law to be obeyed. It was the language of that broader orthodoxy of which Boyse had been so superbly the exponent. Nor is the foregoing an isolated example.

> The Sacrament ... is intended for the most solemn and affectionate declaration that can possibly be made of our love to the Lord Jesus Christ, for the sake of the terms of salvation which he has proposed to us, of our most hearty approbation, and acceptance of these terms, and that it is the established purpose and prevalent disposition of our minds to yield a constant, universal, and cheerful obedience to all his commandments.[39]

In 1735 Abernethy published an interesting sermon, entitled *Persecution contrary to Christianity.* It was delivered on the anniversary of the Irish Rebellion and was directed against the Church of Rome. Against those who argued that the Roman Church contained the vestiges of the true Church, though in a corrupt form, Abernethy denied that the essentials were to be found in her.

> The Papists, 'tis true, profess the fundamental doctrines of Christianity; they profess to believe the Bible which contains them all; and they profess particularly all the articles of the Apostle's Creed. But what does all this amount to more than their having a form of godliness while they deny the power of it?[40]

He then went on to observe:

> ... that salvation is a personal affair...according to men's dispositions, and religious conduct, so shall their condition be by the impartial sentence of their great judge, whatever society they belonged to.[41]

This is almost a doctrine of salvation by works, and might be reinforced by several quotations from this sermon. One more shall suffice:

> From this we may form a just notion of Christianity, and judge of its true design; that it is to improve human nature in moral goodness, to reclaim men from their corrupt dispositions and vicious habits, and make them as like God in all his imitable perfections as it is possible for such creatures to be. Other notions of the gospel-scheme are unworthy. To represent it as intended to distinguish some of mankind from others, by privileges which are

> separable from, and do not ultimately terminate in the perfection of moral rectitude, this is to do it great wrong.[42]

It seems clear then that Abernethy had moved away from the older orthodoxy in his whole doctrine of grace even if he remained orthodox on the deity of Christ, and whatever else he may have regarded as 'the vitals' of Christianity.

This growing trend in Abernethy's theological development is fully evidenced in his later works. Apart from a brief memoir of Craghead, they consist of volumes of his sermons. He published two volumes entitled *Discourses on the Being and Attributes of God.* It was a much admired work in its time, and sought to demonstrate how natural religion and reason necessitated belief in God, and his attributes of spirituality, unity, eternity, omnipotence and omniscience. The texts of the sermons are largely Old Testament texts, and there is little reference to the Christian revelation. The titles themselves indicate the nature of the arguments: they include *The Being of God proved from the Frame of the Material World;* from *Animal and Rational Life;* from *Human Intelligence and Morality; Religion shewn to be perfectly consistent with the true Interest of Mankind.* Abernethy accomplished the remarkable *tour de force* of composing a sermon on the love of God without a single mention of Jesus Christ. In a typical passage he showed the extent to which his thinking had gone in the direction of human goodness and perfectibility:

> ... according to men's notions of the deity, so are their dispositions and their moral conduct; of which the history of all religions: afford us very plain instances. Just sentiments concerning the Supreme Being, as perfectly holy, righteous, and good, tend to produce, and when seriously considered with hearty and pure affection, actually have produced the like tempers and manners in men, carrying human virtue to its greatest height of perfection; whereas the erroneous opinions of many concerning the dispositions of their gods ... have, above all things, corrupted their morals by the desire of imitation, and added the strongest sanction to their vices. Such is the

force and natural operation of love to moral agents... [43]

Two further volumes of sermons were published posthumously in 1757 and went through several editions. These were concerned with practical subjects. Almost the whole of the first volume was devoted to sermons on Proverbs. The second volume included a sermon *Of believing in Jesus Christ*.[44] In this Abernethy set forth his doctrine of justification. This, he held, could never be on the basis of:

> ... base believing, or a naked assent to the truth of Christianity as a divine revelation. It must always be supposed that God dealeth with men according to their moral conduct, and doth not distinguish them by his favour, any otherwise than in proportion to the virtue and goodness which is in their dispositions and behaviour.[45]

He conceded that man cannot by his own efforts merit salvation, or earn acceptance with God. This applied equally to Jew and Gentile, since neither was able to fulfil perfectly the ceremonial or moral law. Jesus by his death, he held, had obtained more favourable terms for us:

> But how are we to understand this? Not as if assent to the truth of the gospel were sufficient instead of obedience to the divine precepts, nor confident reliance on the obedience of Christ, and the merit of his death and passion, which is so to be accounted ours, as if we had fulfilled the law in our own persons; which is not, as far as I can see, any part of the gospel notion of faith ...
>
> ... God hath in great mercy to mankind offered the forgiveness of sins upon most gracious terms; that instead of insisting on an exact conformity to his laws, as the condition of acceptance, which in a more perfect state of human nature might have been highly reasonable, he hath now in great compassion, through Jesus Christ, published a new law, whereby the rigor of the first is abated, and more favourable conditions are proposed. What can the nature of the thing be, but that a less perfect, even a sincere obedience is accepted, such as we are able in this state of infirmity to perform? ... Consequently it is not anything else instead of obedience, any perfect righteous-

> ness imputed to us, by which we are justified ... the terms of it are repentance, and a sincere though imperfect obedience, which I have already shewn you are included in believing; so if we consider the moral perfections of God ... Can it ever enter into our hearts, that he will distinguish them in his regards by considerations entirely foreign to this, or reckon anything to them as their obedience that is not really so?[46]

Abernethy thus emerges as a thorough going neonomian. There is no evidence that his views on the Trinity had altered radically; yet whatever views he may have held on this and on the deity of Christ had become increasingly irrelevant to the main preoccupations of his thought. Set free from the controversy over subscription and from any sense of obligation to the doctrines of the Confession, Abernethy's chief concern was with practical religion, as he himself would have called it, and the constant striving of the individual for the highest degree of obedience to the laws of God, in keeping with the reasonableness and perfection of the whole system of theistic belief.

The main theme of this essay so far has been to examine the doctrinal convictions of John Abernethy in order to determine if his stand for liberty of conscience, especially in the period of the first Subscription Controversy, was in fact a plea for radical departure from the great central doctrines of the faith as Presbyterians have understood them, through the practice of subscription to the Westminster Confession of Faith. It remains finally to attempt a brief survey of Abernethy's opposition to the Test Acts which became a major preoccupation of his struggle for liberty especially in the early 1730s.

The imposition of the Sacramental test in 1704 required every person holding office under the Crown to receive Communion in the established Church within three months of appointment, or forfeit office and be legally disabled from further such appointments. This became a major source of grievance for Presbyterians and they struggled consistently against it. In the period leading up to the Toleration Act of 1719 Presbyterians were involved in discussion among themselves about the terms upon which a legal toleration should be sought. Many felt that only a total acceptance of the Westminster Confession as the basis of their faith would be acceptable. Others would have preferred to draw up some briefer alternative formula. It was against this background that the Belfast Society made known its opposition to any form of subscription to man-made creeds and confessions. One of the reasons why the opposition to Abernethy and his friends was so vehement within the Synod of Ulster was that the suspicion of heterodoxy engendered by their lack of frankness concerning their own theological views was perceived as a serious stumbling block to the full legal toleration which Presbyterians of every shade of opinion so eagerly desired.

The Toleration Act of 1719 had been a bitter disappointment to the Presbyterians. While it had suspended the law against Presbyterian ministers exercising their calling, provided they took an oath of allegiance, and abjured the Pretender and the Pope, it left unchanged the sacramental test for holders of public office. In the years until 1725 the energies of Presbyterians were increasingly diverted to the long and bitter internal struggle over subscription. Some activity did in fact take place upon related questions such as the indemnity of Presbyterian officers in the army, and on the issue of Presbyterian marriages. It was not until 1731 that a new initiative was launched to procure the repeal of the Sacramental Test. A delegation was sent to London to press for action. The Prime Minister, Walpole, was known to favour repeal, and the new Lord Lieutenant, Dorset, was instructed to set the process in motion. In the event he was unable to effect legislation owing to the strong opposition in both Houses of the Irish Parliament.

Among those who lent their voice to the campaign was Abernethy, now living in Dublin. As we have seen, he published tracts entitled *The Nature and Consequences of the Sacramental Test Considered* (1732), and *Reasons for Repeal of the Sacramental* Test (1733). In these two tracts Abernethy attempted a detailed defence of the Presbyterian plea for civil liberty. His basic argument was that the greatest constitutional crises in British history had come about from encroachments by the Crown on the rights of the subject, and that true British patriotism exerted itself in defending and preserving the liberties of the citizen.[47] He held that the Sacramental Test was a political absurdity, since sound government was based upon the light of nature, rather than the Divine revelation, and was the right of all citizens.[48] He denied that the gospel of Christ meddled with the affairs of state, or altered the foundation of civil society, and hence maintained that it was wrong to attempt to secure Church estabishment by incapacitating those who scrupled conformity from their full rights and duties as citizens. To do this, in his view, could not be a proper defence of religion, since people must be given liberty to judge for themselves what were the implications of the gospel, especially in matters controversial.[49]

Abernethy also made a number of interesting practical points in his attack upon the Test Act. He held that it was against the interests of the State to incapacitate so many from its service.[50] If the Sacramental Test was justifiable, then it must equally be right for Roman Catholic nations to penalize their Protestant citizens.[51] He questioned also if those who defended this legislation would support the imposition of a similar test by the established Church of Scotland.[52] Above all he argued that the sacrament was appointed by Christ for spiritual ends, and that it was an abuse of Communion to make it a test of the citizen's loyalty to the State; thus putting at times the worst of men under necessity of receiving the Sacrament regardless of the state of their souls.[53] It would be better by far, he argued, to treat dissenters with kindness, and thus secure their loyalties. He also drew attention to the object-lesson of the Cromwellian Revolution when dissenters overthrew both Crown and Church because, he argued, both had overstepped and abused their powers.[54] Abernethy referred also to the fact that political disability had led large numbers of dissenters to emigrate, thus bringing about a major loss to the Protestant interest. Many dissenters, he argued, played a large part in the trade of the nation, and yet were discouraged from remaining in Ireland.[55]

Abernethy's arguments encapsulated most of what Presbyterians tried to articulate in their opposition to the Sacramental Test. They were presented, however, in the context of his deep convictions about liberty of conscience and were developed with a shrewd instinct for political theory and a wide-ranging knowledge of the constitutional practice of the major European countries. He surveyed this to good account to show the folly of using a spiritual sacrament as a test to judge political loyalty or qualification for office.[56] The attempt to repeal the Test Act in 1731-3 was the last major effort by the Presbyterians to deal with this deeply offensive issue for almost half-a-century. It was not until 1780 that it was finally removed from the statute book. That their efforts to do so failed is no reflection upon the ability with which John Abernethy put their case, crossing swords with Swift in the attempt. He emerged from the struggle with credit, having revealed his characteristic clarity of mind, and gift for persuasive argument.

Abernethy occupied the pulpit of Wood Street with distinction until the end of his life. During his years in Dublin he married a Miss Boyd, who survived him.[57] Some of his daughters married and settled in Antrim, but his son John went to London, where he became a wealthy merchant, and father of Dr John Abernethy, of St Bartholomew's Hospital. Abernethy died of gout at his home in White-Friar Street, close to Wood Street. The date seems to have been 1 December 1740, and he was buried in St Bride's Parish Churchyard on 3 December. The following Sunday memorial sermons were preached, in Wood Street by John Mears, and in Antrim by James Duchal, and both sermons were subsequently published. They pay tribute, as is the custom on such occasions, to the life and work of the deceased. Reading behind the glowing words of adulation one can discern a deep respect for Abernethy as a man of outstanding ability who was 'a great loss to the dissenting interest, yea to the whole Protestant interest in this kingdom'.[58] He:

> was a man of large heart and a catholick spirit, and well understood the principles of the reformation, and the true liberties of men and Christians, and was in every respect

> an ornament of his profession ...[59]

Duchal also referred to the extraordinary respect paid to him, and concluded that he 'had received the adulation of friends to a degree too great for any mortal.[60] Yet he was also described as modest and unassuming. Abernethy was a warm and friendly person, and possessed that rare gift of keeping his temper unruffled and his tongue under control. His love for his congregation is evidenced by his concern on the day before he died that they might find 'a proper person to succeed him'.[61] Tribute was also paid to his deep personal piety. Duchal said of him that 'no man lived more in Heaven ...,' and told of how Abernethy would often withdraw from the world to converse with God.[62]

F. J. Biggar, a descendant of Abernethy's, is somewhat cynical in his estimate:

> The cult of Abernethy in his Wood Street preaching house was ably and consistently maintained, and he had a wide and enlightened following. This is clearly proved by the publication and re-issues of his works from time to time, the expense of their high-class printings, their engravings and their sumptous binding. His *'Discourses'* and *'Postumous Sermons'* were in every library of any repute; his meeting house and residence were ... then in the most fashionable quarter of the Capital ... [63]

Bigger contrasts the full rigour of the law so readily applied to Roman Catholics with the comfortable and relatively secure lot of Abernethy, and his hearers, and draws attention to his many publications, his clothing and portrait, together with the fragments of his library, family silver and other possessions that lingered on.[64] The fact remains, however, that the dissenting Presbyterians suffered considerable hardships and limitations in the early eighteenth century, and were for the most part excluded from the advantages and influence freely enjoyed by members of the established Church. That a man like John Abernethy should have risen to such eminence in an age of adversity is tribute indeed to the gifts and talents with which he was so generously endowed. In the annals of Irish Presbyterianism his reputation is undoubtedly sullied for the part he played in the subscription controversy, and the subsequent rupture in Church policy. Thus, Thomas Witherow concludes that 'there can be no doubt that John Abernethy of Antrim is the true father of the Freethinking School of Irish Presbyterians.'[65]

> He was a man of pure moral character, great industry, scholarly tastes and superior talents, but it must ever be regretted that his influence was so injurious to the Church of which he should have been the support and the ornament.[66]

The judgement is harsh, yet there can be little doubt that Abernethy's fixation with the principle of liberty during the period of the subscription controversy led him to upset and trouble many sincere Presbyterian people when he could so easily have allayed their fears by the frank and open assertion of belief in the fundamental doctrines of the faith. It is best to judge him as the child of his time, who somewhat in advance of many of his contemporaries had imbibed the new confidence in man and his achievements that was to be the hallmark of the eighteenth century. It was the spirit of an age which, while manifesting much that was great, had drifted from its theological moorings. Abernethy's impatience with dogmatic theology was to find many sympathisers among Presbyterians, and not only non-subscribers, but subscribers also, as the century progressed. In the long run, however, it failed to attract the mind and heart of the Church. The heirs of Abernethy and the non-subscribers were eventually, for the most part, to adopt a unitarian position, and thus place themselves outside orthodox Christian theology. With the benefit of hindsight, it is scarcely surprising to find Abernethy so little valued today in the Church he served. Yet he remains an important figure in its history who represented with great ability a viewpoint cherished by many in his time, caught up in the tension between freedom and formulary that, in one form or another, will be debated again and again.

OWEN ROE O'NEILL

c.1582–1649

Soldier and Politician

Raymond Gillespie

OWEN ROE O'NEILL

On 6 November 1649 Owen Roe O'Neill died at Cloughoughter Castle, the home of his brother-in-law, Myles O'Reilly, about seven miles west of Cavan town.[1] Present at his death bed were his son, his personal physician, Owen O'Sheil, the Archbishop of Armagh and the Bishop of Kilmore. His wife, Rosa O'Doherty, was not there, arriving from Galway a few days later. The former Commander of the Ulster forces of the Confederated Catholics of Ireland was even separated from the remnants of his army, camped around Mullingar. His death, probably from tetanus, although later tradition insisted that he had been poisoned, was not unexpected. He had been seriously ill since early August and had arrived at Cloughoughter on a litter as he was unable to ride. It was not an inspiring end for one whose public image as a military commander had stood high in Ireland in the 1640s.

Owen Roe's death was in stark contrast to the tumultuous welcome he had received when he landed at Doe Castle in north Donegal on 6 July 1642. Born in Armagh in the 1580s, he had gone to the Spanish Netherlands as a soldier in 1604 or early 1605. When the Ulster gentry rose on 22 October 1641 in response to political, economic and social difficulties to which they could see only a military solution, Owen began to make preparations to return to Ireland. While he was certainly aware that a rising was being planned he did not intend his return to coincide with it. Much of the time between October 1641 and July 1642 he spent trying to raise arms and obtain permission to leave his regiment in the Spanish Netherlands. This was never granted and it was technically as a deserter that he arrived in Ulster.[2] He was warmly welcomed on his arrival. He marched from Donegal Castle and arrived at Tynan church in Co. Tyrone on 18 July 1642 where he was greeted by the leader of the Ulster insurgents, Sir Phelim O'Neill; and on 29 August he attended a general assembly of the Ulster Irish at Clones which acknowledged him as commander. Owen Roe's standing was already high in Ulster. Many of the settlers whose versions of the events of late 1641 and 1642 were recorded in depositions noted that the natives boasted that Owen, who had established a considerable military reputation on the Continent, would return to help them. Movement between Ulster and the Spanish Netherlands was common in the early seventeenth century. Franciscan friars moved to and from the Franciscan college at Louvain and the armies of the Spanish Netherlands provided a career outlet for the younger sons of many of the native landowning families of Ulster. Through these channels Owen's military achievements were well known in Ulster and he must have appeared an obvious source of supplies and assistance to the native Irish.

Such a military leader was badly needed in mid-1642. The rising had begun as a conservative affair intended to put the gentry of Ulster in a strong bargaining position with the Dublin administration, but the plan had gone wrong.[3] The war had gone on longer than the plotters had envisaged and had become more radical than its initial conservative aims. The force had pushed out of Ulster, besieging Drogheda in November 1641, and in December had forced the Catholic Old English of the Pale to join it. Much of this success was reversed by the raising of the siege of Drogheda in March 1642, the defeat of the insurgents at Kilrush in Co. Kildare in April, and the arrival at Carrickfergus in the same month of Robert Munroe with a Scottish army to reinforce the settlers. When Owen Roe arrived the Ulster forces were about to surrender but his presence injected a new vitality into the situation. Two months later Thomas Preston, Owen Roe's rival for military preferment on the Continent, arrived at Wexford with further men and supplies. Alongside these military developments the insurgents had also begun to organise themselves politically. In May 1642 Catholic clergy and laity met at Kilkenny and the so-called Confederation of Kilkenny, based on an oath of association, was born. Its first formal meeting was held in late October and November 1642.[4]

Since the Confederation was intended to be the coordinating body for the military and political activities of the insurgents, Owen Roe needed to be recognised by it as a military commander. On 13 November, after a short campaign season against Munroe's forces which achieved little, he left Ulster for Kilkenny. However, even in its first session tensions were becoming apparent within the Confederation. On the one hand the Old English, loyal to the King in temporal matters but allowing the Pope supremacy in spiritual matters, wanted to end the war as soon as possible by making an agreement with the King's representative, the Lord Deputy, the Earl of Ormond. The outlook of the Old English was essentially conservative and their tactics derived from their experience in Parliament. Many of the native Irish on the other hand wished to prolong the war, seeing it as their only bargaining counter with the New English administration in Ireland. They could thus extract further concessions on the interrelated matters of landownership and religious toleration. Part of this more radical attitude stemmed from the manner in which the Counter Reformation had been promoted in early seventeenth-century Ireland. Among the Old English of the Pale there prevailed a rather conservative structure of secular clergy whose observance of the details of the decrees of the Council of Trent was often perfunctory. In Gaelic Ireland, however, regular clergy from the religious orders, especially the Franciscans, were in a clear majority. These latter clergy had been trained in the Continental colleges, especially at Louvain, in the rigid ideas of the Counter Reformation and their return to Ireland had promoted the radicalisation of the native Irish in the years before 1641. Franciscan friars were prominent both during the early years of the rising in Ulster and later in the forces of the Confederation.[5] What many native Irish no doubt wished was to see the Confederation established as the permanent government of Ireland; whereas the Old English saw it as a temporary expedient which had no claims to usurp the legitimate government of Ireland vested in the King and the Irish Parliament.

Owen Roe's expectation of the Confederation's role is clear. His Continental background and his power base in Ulster certainly inclined him towards the native Irish view. The view of the Confederation among the native Irish in Continental Europe was set out in a letter from Hugh Bourke, the Commissary of the Franciscans in Belgium, to Luke Wadding. Describing the Confederates' oath, he noted it was 'intended solely to secure the constancy of all in the defence of the [Catholic] faith to the very last man. By these laws it is manifest how purely this war of Ireland is for the defence and propagation of the Catholic faith without admission of any other motive.'[6] However, within the Confederation the Old English were numerically and tactically superior to the native Irish. They succeeded in dominating the events of the General Assembly and Supreme Council of the Confederation and repeatedly pressed for peace. It is significant that most of those who represented Ulster in the Confederation were the less radical of the Ulster Irish. Sir Phelim O'Neill, for example, was not a member of the General Assembly until 1646: that session was dominated by the radical clerical party led by the papal nuncio, Rinuccini.

Owen Roe was probably not fully aware of the subtleties of Confederation politics when he left Kilkenny to return to Ulster, arriving at Charlemont, Co. Armagh on 6 January 1643. The military situation in Ulster posed more pressing problems. Owen Roe had spent most of his life as a soldier in the well organised army of the Spanish Netherlands and was a recognised expert in the tactics of the set piece battle and the use of the pike, which were integral elements in the dramatic changes which formed the 'military revolution' of early modern Europe.[7] He was also an acknowledged expert in siege warfare. All of these skills were of little use in Ireland. There were few large towns to besiege and in any case he had few cannon or supplies to undertake a siege. The accepted tactics were those of guerilla warfare which had characterised the Nine Years War almost forty years earlier. Indeed the 1640s saw many of the old fortifications from this war, such as the crannog (a fortified man-made island), brought back into use after being abandoned for forty years. The force with which Owen had to deal had been recently formed and was untrained, and Sir Phelim O'Neill who commanded it had no military experience. The force had been raised in an *ad hoc* way, each family under Sir Phelim's influence contributing a group of men. Thus after the siege of Drogheda, 'the Ulstermen departed ... the chief of every family with their proper parties went to their several counties'. The command structure was weak and much was left to the personal influence of the heads of families. The result was often chaotic. Owen described the force he found as an undisciplined rabble which committed cruelties, 'such as are not usual even among Moors and Arabs'; there was 'no obedience among soldiers, if one [can] call men soldiers who behave nothing better than animals'.[8] The loose command structure meant that it was difficult to hold the army together or to ensure that rendezvous were met. Many of the native Irish took a short-term view of the war effort and after battles it was difficult to maintain the momentum of any victory gained. One contemporary explanation of Owen Roe's failure to follow up the victory of Benburb was that 'the Catholics, all now grown rich, dispersed to a large extent, each one anxious to return to his own home with the booty that had fallen to his share — a practice by no means rare when the conquerors' homes are not too remote from the scene of their victory'. Given this irregular organisation, it is hardly surprising that Owen did not have the sort of back-up facilities in terms of supply to which he was used from campaigns on the Continent.[9] His Connacht campaign of 1647, for example, was ruined by lack of supplies and the Scottish force which he was to contain broke out of the province to reinforce the Parliamentary force in Leinster, which inflicted a severe defeat on the Confederate forces at the battle of Dungans Hill in August 1647. As a result war in Ireland proved a disillusioning experience for a man skilled in the techniques of Continental warfare and within weeks of his arrival in Ulster he was considering returning to Flanders.

With all these military and organisational problems it is hardly surprising that Owen's first full campaigning season in 1643 was an inauspicious one. The early part of the year was taken up with a series of skirmishes between the native Irish forces and the Scottish forces under the command of Robert Munroe in east Ulster, and with Sir Robert Stewart's force of settlers in the Laggan in Co. Donegal. Owen was soon outmanoeuvered and forced to make a series of tactical retreats which ended disastrously at the battle of Clones in June 1643.[10] Owen lost a number of experienced officers who had come with him from Flanders, his force was scattered and supplies lost. The remainder of the force had to retreat westward into Leitrim and later into Roscommon to regroup. This gave Owen a chance to begin training the remnants of his force in the techniques of warfare with which he was familiar and his march into Co. Meath later in the year was more successful. He seized Portlester castle, about six miles west of Trim, and defeated the Dublin government's force under Lord Moore at Athboy. Owen made good use of his cannon and began to use the tactics typical of Continental warfare but was unable to develop them. On 15 September 1643 the Earl of Castlehaven arrived at Owen Roe's camp to inform him that a one-year cessation had been agreed between the Confederation and the Lord Deputy, the Earl of Ormond.

Negotiations for a cessation to allow time for the discussion of a peace treaty had been going on since January. However, it was not welcomed by all parties. The Dublin administration had misgivings about negotiating with men whom they regarded as rebels; and the papal envoy, Father Scarampi, who had arrived in July 1643, also had doubts about a cessation with 'heretics' in what he saw as a religious war. Owen accepted the cessation and retreated to Ulster. There, however, the situation was confused. A year earlier civil war had broken out in England between King and Parliament. Robert Munroe's forces in Ulster were paid by the English Parliament, which ordered him not to accept a cessation with rebels which had been negotiated with the King's representative. The settler forces in Ulster initially accepted the cessation but by the end of 1643 were so short of supplies that they were forced to accept the Solemn League and Covenant and join with Munroe in continuing the war.[11] Thus, Owen was left fighting a campaign in Ulster. In 1644 the Confederation decided to send a special expedition against the force in Ulster. However, the Old English element in the Confederation distrusted O'Neill and appointed the Earl of Castlehaven as their commander. The expedition was a disaster. Poor communications, lack of supplies and missed rendezvous dogged it from the start. O'Neill seems to have had problems in mustering his forces and his men all dispersed, according to Castlehaven, 'everyone looking to save what he had'. Moreover, Castlehaven's final comment on events rather sinisterly noted 'the failing or something else of General Owen Roe O'Neill'.[12] Owen Roe took the failure badly. In February 1645, for example, he was offering to return to the Continent with levies of Ulstermen to fight in Spanish Flanders, but his proposal was unacceptable to Philip IV of Spain.[13] No further concerted campaign was launched in Ulster until 1646 when Owen led another force into the province. This time the army was better organised and Owen had had a chance to prepare his men during the spring of 1646, with special emphasis on weapons training. As a result this was a much more successful campaign, culminating in Owen's defeat of Robert Munroe at Benburb on 6 June. The victory was the result of a combination of factors. O'Neill had managed to assemble a force which he could at last deploy in a type of warfare of which he was master, not least in regard to the use of the pike. On the other side Munroe's force was badly weakened by desertions and lack of supplies. One contemporary recorded that Munroe's soldiers were so weak from hunger that they could not even push a pike.[14] Yet Owen was not able to follow up the victory. Desertions from his own force, happy to have won a battle, and political circumstances undermined his temporary success.

Owen Roe's victory at Benburb was overshadowed by deepening tensions in the Confederation at Kilkenny. Following the cessation of 1643, negotiations began over a more lasting peace. Charles I sent a personal envoy, the Earl of Glamorgan, to continue negotiations and a secret treaty was concluded in August 1645. The treaty was not to the liking of the Papal Nuncio in Ireland, Giovanni Rinuccini, Archbishop of Fermo, who arrived in October 1645.[15] Rinuccini dictated new terms which were unacceptable to

Lord Deputy Ormond, and Glamorgan was arrested although subsequently released. Peace was not finally agreed until March 1646 and proclaimed in Dublin on 30 July. Rinuccini condemned the peace as making insufficient provision for the supremacy of the Catholic Church under the new order. He summoned a Synod at Waterford in August which laid an interdict on all places accepting the peace and excommunicated all those who did likewise. Owen's reactions to these events are significant. In April 1646 he argued that 'it were better for us to have absolute wars than a corrupted cessation' and referred to the agreement as a 'vile treaty' which could not guarantee the freedom of the country because of the lack of provisions for religion.[16] It was to Rinuccini, rather than the Confederation, that Owen Roe reported his success at Benburb; Rinuccini sent his secretary, Father Massari, to discuss the situation; and Owen offered to march on Kilkenny if the Nuncio wished. Owen marched south towards Kilkenny in August 1646 and provided support for Rinuccini who deposed the Supreme Council and replaced it with one under his own presidency. In the face of such pressure the remainder of the Confederate army under Thomas Preston joined Owen's forces. The fragility of this alliance was revealed in late 1646 when the combined force marched on Dublin. Lack of supplies and personal rivalry between the two commanders reduced the expedition to a fiasco. Owen retreated from the city, realising that he had little hope of taking it by siege, and Preston promptly entered into negotiation with the Earl of Clanricard, subsequently signing a modified version of the Ormond peace on 19 November. According to Clanricard's version of events he even had Sir Phelim O'Neill's support. Owen and Rinuccini were forced to retreat to Kilkenny.

Owen Roe's actions in 1646 raise a number of important questions about his motivation for being in Ireland. While relations between the Old English and the native Irish within the Confederation were tense, Owen Roe's breach with the Confederation over the peace of 1646 was so decisive and his alliance with Rinuccini so absolute, when even apparently Sir Phelim fell away, that more than simple racial antagonism must have been involved. The events of 1646 can only be understood in the context of his experience before he arrived in Ireland. Owen was born in the early 1580s, the youngest son of Art McBaron O'Neill, lord of the territory of Oneilland in north Armagh and half-brother to the Earl of Tyrone. Given his position in the family, Owen had little outlet for ambition. The most he might have aspired to was service as a swordsman among his father's or elder brother's followers. He was in a similar position to that of the three sons of Turlough McHenry O'Neill of the Fews in south Armagh who, according to Sir Robert Jacob in 1609, were swordsmen in their father's house.[17] Native Irish society in the sixteenth century had a use for such men since it was articulated by cattle raiding and warfare, and a man's status was measured by the number of his followers. With the restructuring of society in the early seventeenth century, under which a man's status was measured by his landholding and legal position rather than by the number of his followers, such men became redundant. One obvious outlet for the redundant swordsmen was the armies of Continental Europe, especially in Flanders where the Spanish were at war with the Dutch. All three sons of Turlough O'Neill of the Fews, for example, served in the Spanish forces.

In late 1604 or early 1605 Owen Roe was serving in the Irish contingent of the Spanish forces in Flanders. By 1606 one of Owen's elder brothers, Art, was serving as a captain in Henry O'Neill's regiment and by 1609 one of his cousins was also in Europe.[18] Owen was to spend forty years as a soldier of fortune in the army of Spanish Flanders. His experience was not altogether a happy one. In 1609 his company was dissolved as part of the reorganisation of the Spanish army following the truce of Antwerp in 1609. He considered returning home but in 1611 he rejoined the regiment as sergeant-major. His ability was overshadowed by the political necessity of accommodating the descendants of the Earls of Tyrone and Tyrconnell, who were usually in dispute over precedence. Certainly by the 1630s Owen was becoming increasingly dissatisfied with his lot. In January 1632 Hugh O'Donnell, the young Earl of Tyrconnell, was given his own regiment which upset Owen considerably since he did not receive a commission until the next year, and then only after complaint. In 1634 he wrote to an agent in Ireland: 'I am mighty troubled and have few to assist me and many that get things here ought not to get them more than you might'.[19] This discontent was probably a significant factor in his decision to leave the Spanish army without permission to return to Ireland in 1642. Significantly, one of the arguments used to persuade Owen to do so was intended to appeal to his dissatisfaction. Hugh McPhelim O'Byrne, one of O'Neill's officers, argued as follows during the siege at Arras in 1641: 'we are to adventure our lives for the succouring of a scabbed town of the King of Spain where we may happily lose our lives' — mutinous sentiments, unless the commander happened to agree with them.[20]

While there were disappointments, the situation of the Irish community in the Spanish Netherlands was a formative influence on Owen Roe's attitudes. That community had been growing gradually from the 1580s when Sir William Stanley brought the first large military unit of Irishmen to Flanders as part of the Earl of Leicester's expedition. The flow of immigrants had increased with the effects of war in Ireland during the 1590s. The end of the war in 1603 provided opportunity for recruiting for the Spanish armies among both native Irish and Old English. The Dublin government was keen to remove those who had been involved in the war who they felt would be a potentially disruptive force. As early as 1601 Lord Deputy Mountjoy wrote: 'there needs little now to settle this kingdom but some way to rid the idle swordsmen of both sides'.[21] Levies for Flanders began in 1605, made possible by peace agreed between England and Spain in 1604, and Irish were also sent to Sweden. This was not enforced emigration, as many Irish saw little future in Ireland and were happy to go abroad, often as members of family groups. Younger sons often saw more future for themselves in military careers abroad than at home. Moreover, emigration was not permanent. There was considerable movement between the Continent and Ireland as men were recruited and then retired to Ireland after a number of years service. By the end of 1607 the Irish regiment in Flanders stood at about 1,700 men. One of the most important aspects of that group was that while they integrated into the local community to some degree they also kept a strong sense of a separate Irish identity.[22] In towns such as Brussels and Bruges distinct Irish quarters emerged. Within the army Irish companies had been established by 1596, and a separate Irish regiment under the command of Henry O'Neill, the son of the Earl of Tyrone, was set up in 1605. This force was not entirely Irish but it was mainly so. The separate identity of the Irish community was also reflected in the fact that Irish continued to be spoken. Owen Roe himself communicated through letters in Irish with those at home. Some soldiers, it was reported, could speak only Irish and had little or no Spanish, French or Flemish. Some native Irish went so far as to maintain the traditional trappings of lordship society while they were abroad, including patronising poets and maintaining their genealogy. It would be wrong to overstress this trend. There was intermarriage between the Irish and the inhabitants of Spanish Flanders as well as other contacts, such as choosing godparents for their children from local inhabitants.

While at the social level there may have been strong lines of continuity between life in Ireland and in Spanish Flanders, in other areas, notably ideas on religion and politics, there was little common ground between the Irish at home and those with Continental experience. Life in Continental Europe exposed Irish emigrants to a wide range of political and religious ideas which had not yet penetrated Ireland. In the area of political thought, for example, they began to experiment with new ideas of political organisation. A case in point is the proposed plan for the invasion of Ireland which was developed by Owen Roe and others at Louvain in the years between 1625 and 1627, when Anglo-Spanish relations were at a low ebb following the failure of the Spanish match between the son of James I, the future Charles I, and the daughter of Philip IV. The idea of Ireland which the plotters developed was set out in a memorandum of 1627 which envisaged that the enterprise was to be carried out 'in the name of liberty of the fatherland and of oppressed religion and by establishing as the government a Republic, which should be so called on its flags and its commissions and all other public ordinances should be in the name of the Republic and kingdom of Ireland.'[23] The Earls of Tyrone and Tyrconnell were to be joint captains-general, one commanding on land and the other at sea. This was an attempt to solve the problem of who was to be supreme commander, a continual source of contention between them. The gentry were to make themselves masters of their provinces and 'each of the nobles, provinces or principal entities which shall have taken part in the insurrection shall name deputies who will attend the headquarters of the army or Court to vote the measures or assessments which shall have been decided upon'. There was to be no King since their aim was 'not to conquer the country for any other prince or for the Earls [of Tyrone and Tyrconnell] themselves but for the kingdom and Republic of Ireland'. In the longer term 'time and events will show whatever else must be done'. In the event the plan was stillborn since Philip IV refused to accept it: 'he had no intention of acquiring any new dominion for his crown', despite the fact that this was not the aim of the plan.

What is significant is that Owen Roe and others were using the models of political organisation which they found on the Continent to devise plans for Ireland. In this case the model was the Dutch republic which the Spanish had failed to conquer despite a sustained campaign. Florence Conry, although Archbishop of Tuam, spent most of his life in Spain and at Louvain in the Spanish Netherlands and noted the strength of this republican organisation in January 1627, 'although they [the Dutch] defend an unjust cause as rebels against God [being Protestant] and their lawful prince'. The Irish, by contrast, were fighting for the godly cause of Catholicism.[24] Such views were out of line with developments in Ireland where many of the native Irish and Old English accepted the King as their lawful secular ruler: the rebellion of 1641 was not against the King but rather in support of him against his 'evil counsellors', the Puritan faction. At Louvain the Franciscans were developing another idea, that of a separate historical kingdom of Ireland with an illustrious past which continued to the present. While the strict constitutional position of Ireland was that of a kingdom, following the 1541 Act making Henry VIII monarch of a separate kingdom of Ireland, the institutions of the kingdom — the Privy Council, the Parliament, local government and the established church — had fallen into the hands of Protestant colonists who regarded Ireland as inferior and subject to the crown of England. The Louvain idea was a kingdom in which the Catholics of Ireland would establish a Catholic commonwealth and in which the established church would be the Catholic Church, although they never resolved the problem of a Catholic kingdom governed by a Protestant monarch. This was the idea which Owen Roe seems to have adopted on his return in 1642, regarding the Confederation as the new government of a separate kingdom with Charles as its King. By 1645, however, he had modified this position by suggesting that the King should be Philip IV of Spain, and he offered to occupy Ireland on his behalf.[25] Most of Owen Roe's disputes with the Old-English-dominated Confederation were to relate to the role of the church in the state.

If Owen Roe absorbed many of the political ideas of Continental Europe, he also absorbed the religious ideas which were current there. Those who settled in Spanish Flanders soon came in contact with the ideas of Counter Reformation Catholicism which had not yet made a significant impact on much of Ireland. As the English Ambassador in Brussels, Thomas Edmonds, observed in 1606, the Irish were 'a people, though for the most part ignorant, yet generally addicted to superstition, which by means of these foreign services they would be more and more mislead in it.'[26] His fears were well-founded: each company of soldiers in the Irish regiment had a chaplain and in 1606 Hugh MacCaughwell, the head of the Irish College at Louvain, was appointed Chaplain-in-Chief, and from then on the post was held by the Guardian of the College. The College itself was established in 1606 as one of the growing number of Irish Colleges on the Continent for the education of Catholics. It was attached to the University of Louvain which had been one of the staunchest promoters of the Counter Reformation and whose theologians had a prominent part in the Council of Trent. Much work was done in the College during the early seventeenth century in producing materials, such as catechisms and devotional literature, for the promotion of the Counter Reformation in Ireland. The Irish Franciscans in Louvain were also concerned to demonstrate the antiquity of the Catholic Church as the true church in Ireland through the writing of the lives of the saints, just as back in Ireland Archbishop Ussher was attempting to demonstrate the antiquity of the Church of Ireland. Owen Roe spent much of his life in Louvain when not on campaign. He absorbed many of the ideas of Louvain and, significantly, before the battle of Benburb he told his men to fight for their birthright 'and for the religion which your forefathers professed and maintained since Christianity came first to this land'.[27] He was intimately associated with the clergy at Louvain and one of his patrons was Florence Conry, one of the Guardians of the College, who had petitioned Hugh O'Neill, the Earl of Tyrone, in 1610 for Owen Roe to be the commander of Henry O'Neill's regiment after Henry's death. Owen soon became part of what has been described as a 'northern clique' at Louvain, which also included Robert Chamberlain and Eugene Mathews, the Archbishop of Dublin. One of the central ideas with which these men dealt was the nationalism which the Counter Reformation produced by identifying the fate of Ireland with the fate of the Counter Reformation Catholic Church. This was a familiar theme among those from Europe who arrived in Ireland. Monsignor Massari, Rinucinni's secretary, for example, referred to those who rejected the Earl of Ormond as 'the true lovers of faith and fatherland'.[28]

The reaction of Irish emigrants on the Continent to these ideas was mixed. Owen Roe, it is clear, absorbed them fully. In a letter to Nicholas French, Bishop of Ferns, in 1646, Owen Roe declared himself 'for the Catholic Church and the freedom of my country'; and when Monsignor Massari visited Owen Roe's camp in the aftermath of the battle of Benburb he described Owen and his Continentally-trained officers as 'profoundly Catholic and faithful to the Holy See and to the sovereign pontiff'. It was the health of Innocent X which was drunk on that occasion. Owen had also promised Massari that he 'was ready to serve in the common cause of God, religion and country in any manner the Nuncio would indicate'.[29] For others on the Continent the situation was not so clear cut. The intertwining of politics and religion was not as straightforward a matter for many of the Old English on the Continent. Unlike the native Irish many had strong connections and land at home and were still strongly influenced by developments there. Many of the Old English in Ireland had developed a sophisticated political outlook which divorced religion and politics. The King would claim their temporal allegiance and the Pope their spiritual allegiance. In some ways such a view was untenable in a situation in which the King was also head of the Anglican Church. To refuse the King spiritual allegiance was to undermine his secular authority. Yet, for the Old English, loyalty to the King was essential as a supreme court of appeal against the New English administration in Ireland. Not surprisingly there was tension between the Old English and native Irish on the Continent. In 1608, for example, Thomas Preston, whose relations with Owen Roe were poor, argued against Henry O'Neill that 'it was not lawful, neither would he ever bear arms against his sovereign'. Preston's view of the events of the 1640s was that he was 'promoting the interests of religion, King and country'.[30] These men found it difficult to adapt to new ideas especially since their fathers and brothers still maintained others at home. Many natives had no such family contact with home and absorption of new ideas was less difficult. The division between the Old English and the native Irish was, admittedly, not clear cut. There were many Old English who accepted the new ideas and some native Irish who did not, but broadly speaking there was a clear tension between the political ideas implicit in the Counter Reformation and the ideas of the Old English community abroad which was never resolved. It was most acute among the Old English clergy who were pulled between the ideas of their community and those of their Church.

Many of the theological and devotional ideas of the Counter Reformation were slow to reach Ireland. Rinuccini was dismayed at the state of religion in the country and wrote to Rome of the dismal state of Catholicism.[31] Many of the clear lines of division which were developed in Louvain lost their meaning in the realities of an Irish context and the normally sharp distinction between heretic and Catholic was often blurred. Rinuccini himself was shocked by a conversation with a Munsterman, whom he described as 'a very good Catholic', about whether a force from Ulster could be used in Munster or not: 'I suggested that, after all, it was better to have Catholics than heretics in the province; he replied with great effrontery and without the least hesitation that this was not always the case'.[32] Men like Rinuccini and his followers had great difficulty in understanding the position of the Old English of the Confederation as summed up in its motto: '*pro Deo, pro Patria et pro Rego*'. The war for him, and for Owen Roe, was not about restoring the *status quo* but about setting up a new kingdom which would be a Catholic commonwealth.

Thus, forty years in Europe in close contact with the ideas of the Counter Reformation, which had not yet penetrated Ireland, had estranged Owen Roe from the realities of Irish politics. Just as he found an army untrained in the Continental methods of warfare so he found a political tradition which was not that with which he had lived for most of his life. Naturally his reaction was to align himself with that faction which most represented his own political and religious outlook. That faction was headed by the Continental prelate Rinuccini. Further evidence of his allegiance to that party is provided by the events surrounding the Inchiquin peace of 1648 which were a near repetition of those of 1646. On 20 May 1648 the Confederation concluded a truce with the Earl of Inchiquin who, although Parliamentary commander in Munster, was negotiating with Ormond. Rinuccini issued a censure of excommunication against anyone accepting the truce but unlike 1646 he did not have the military strength to support his decree.[33] Owen Roe's army had become increasingly discontented during 1647 and 1648. In 1647 he had lost regiments through a mutiny when men had refused to participate in the Leinster campaign against the newly arrived forces of the English Parliament. Significantly, the five regiments which mutinied were not commanded by officers with Continental experience and they failed to understand what Owen's aims were. Again, during 1648 other mutinies developed among the Ulster force, fomented by, among others, Sir Phelim O'Neill.[34] The attempted excommunication by the Nuncio was resisted by the Confederates in a much more forceful way than had been the case in 1646. On a diplomatic level they appealed to Rome and the dispute over the validity of the excommunication spread into Europe.[35] On a more practical level Owen Roe's command was rescinded and on 30 September he was proclaimed a traitor by the Confederation who accused him of assisting the Parliamentary forces to plan an attack on Kilkenny. This outright breach with the Confederation was compounded by the negotiation of a peace treaty between Ormond and the Confederation following Ormond's return to Ireland in September, after having been in England for negotiations with the King. The treaty was concluded on 17 January 1649. Thirteen days later Charles I was executed in England. The terms of the treaty were similar to that of 1646 and Owen refused to recognise it.

For Owen Roe these events were of limited significance compared with the departure from Ireland of Rinuccini on 25 February 1649. Convinced that he had failed in his main mission of firmly establishing the Catholic Church in Ireland on a Continental model, Rinuccini sailed from Galway. Owen Roe was now almost totally isolated in Ireland. There were few left who understood and shared his ideas. Cast adrift, Owen began negotiations with both Cromwell and the Council of State in England and, through Fathers Patrick Crelly and Francis Nugent, with the exiled Charles II. He also began negotiations with the Parliamentary commanders at Dublin and in Ulster, Michael Jones, Charles Coote and George Monck. He also aided Monck at Dundalk and assisted at the relief of Derry in July. On 8

May he agreed a cessation with the army of Parliament but the Parliament in England condemned it. Even under such stress the ideas of Counter Reformation Catholicism were still strong and he wrote to Pope Innocent X justifying his action. He had more success in negotiations with the Earl of Ormond. He continued to insist that the Catholic Church had not been given enough guarantees in the treaties of 1646 and 1649. Ormond capitulated and on 12 October 1649 articles for a treaty were put together and agreed on 20 October. Seventeen days later Owen Roe died.

The experience of Owen Roe in seventeenth-century Ireland was a strange one. His seven years in Ireland must be seen in the context of the previous forty years which he had spent outside the country. He was a military commander of considerable skill and ability in Europe but in Ireland most of his military activities were inconclusive. The ideas of Continental Europe, whether military, political or religious, were often inappropriate to the reality of the Irish situation. As a result Owen Roe soon found himself isolated in Ireland, clinging only to those who best understood him, the Continentally-trained clergy. Even his apparent natural allies, the native Irish of Ulster who supported him through most of the 1640s, had deserted him by the time of his death. When he died he was unmourned by the traditional native poets but, significantly, an elegy was composed by an anonymous poet about 1650, not in Ireland but in Rome. The poet, whose lament recorded Owen's great military successes of the 1640s, enumerated his good qualities and concluded that Cromwell, who landed in Ireland almost three months before Owen Roe's death, would not have had success in Ireland had Owen Roe lived.[36] By the standards of Ireland, Owen's intervention had been a failure but by the standards of Counter Reformation Europe it had been a principled act.

NOTES AND REFERENCES

1

B. CATHCART

ERNEST WALTON:

Atomic Scientist, 1903–

1 *Nature*, 30 April 1932.

2 Quoted in Sir M. Oliphant, *Rutherford: Recollections of the Cambridge Days* (London, 1972), p.88.

3 R. Nichols & M. Browne, *Wings over Europe* (London, 1932), p.90.

4 *Irish Times*, 16 Nov 1951.

5 Recollections of Physics at Trinity College, Dublin in the 1920s, in *The Making of Physicists*, ed. R. Williamson, (London, 1987), p.46.

6 R. B. McDowell & D. A. Webb, Trinity College Dublin: *An Academic History*, (Cambridge, 1982), p.456.

7 G. Hartcup & T. E. Allibone, *Cockcroft and the Atom* (London, 1984), p.39.

8 Ibid. p.43.

9 *Irish Times*, 11 April 1982.

10 *Daily Mirror*, 3 May 1932.

11 *Manchester Guardian*, 2 May 1932.

12 Hartcup & Allibone, op. cit. p.164.

2

T. G. FRASER

CLAUDE AUCHINLECK:

Military Leader, 1884–1981

I am glad to acknowledge the courtesy of the late Field-Marshal Sir Claude Auchinleck for responding so generously to my queries about his career and about the Indian Army. He asked that he should not be quoted or have his observations attributed and I have respected this. My thanks are also due to the late General Sir Reginald Savory, Adjutant-General-in-India, 1946-1947, and formerly of the 14th (Ferozepore) Sikhs. I must also thank the staff of the John Rylands Library, University of Manchester, for their courtesy when I consulted the Auchinleck Papers and the Faculty of Humanities of the University of Ulster for financial assistance.

1 For his ancestry and family background, see J. Connell, *Auchinleck* (London, 1959), pp.3-6.

2 Churchill's views are in *My Early Life* (London, 1930). He retained an ambivalent view of India and those connected with its affairs.

3 See Connell, op. cit. pp.31-50.

4 Ibid. pp.72-3.

5 Ibid. pp.87-150; W. S. Churchill, *The Second World War*, i (London, 1948), pp.514-5.

6 M. Gilbert, *Winston S. Churchill*, vi (London, 1983), p.661.

7 Connell, op. cit. p.153.

8 Churchill, *The Second World War*, iii (London, 1950), p.237.

9 Gilbert, op. cit. p.1115.

10 Rommel's career has been well covered in D. Young, *Rommel* (London, 1950), to which Auchinleck contributed the Foreword, and in B. H. Liddell Hart (ed), *The Rommel*

Papers (London, 1953).

11 Young, op. cit. p.105.

12 Auchinleck to Churchill, 14 July 1942, Auchinleck Papers, MUL 980.

13 Gilbert, op. cit. vi, p.1192-3.

14 Connell, op. cit. p.270-304.

15 Ibid. pp.357-71; it is useful to compare the near-contemporary official account in *The Eighth Army* (London, 1944).

16 Liddell Hart, op. cit. pp.173-180.

17 See e.g. Sir John Dill to Auchinleck, 9 July 1942, Auchinleck Papers, MUL 974.

18 Connell, op. cit. pp.565-92; Liddell Hart, op. cit. pp.228-32.

19 Churchill, *The Second World War*, iv (London, 1951), pp.343-4.

20 Auchinleck to Churchill, 24 June 1942, Auchinleck Papers, MUL 953.

21 Auchinleck to Brooke, 28 June 1942, Auchinleck Papers, MUL 961a; Liddell Hart, op. cit. p.249.

22 Liddell Hart, op. cit. p.257.

23 There are many accounts of these events. J. Connell gives Auchinleck's version in *Auchinleck*, pp.691-722. Churchill's account is in *The Second World War*, iv, pp.408-24. His letter of 8 August 1942 may be seen in the Auchinleck Papers, MUL 990; it is endorsed as having been received at 8th Army HQ El Alamein. A useful 'outsider's' account is that of Lord Moran in Winston Churchill, *The Struggle for Survival 1940-1965* (London, 1966), pp.46-53. Montgomery's version is in his *Memoirs* (London, 1958), pp.91-106. His assessment may be compared with that of Rommel in Liddell Hart, *The Rommel Papers*, p.260.

24 Montgomery's comments may be found in Gilbert, 'Never Despair', *Winston S. Churchill 1945-1965* (London, 1988), p.420; Lord Linlithgow to L. S. Amery, 19 June 1943, N. Mansergh (ed) *The Transfer of Power 1942-7*, iv (London, 1973), pp.14-22.

25 G. Brooke-Shepherd, 'The Silent Warrior with Much to Tell', *Sunday Telegraph*, 29 March 1981.

26 Note by Field-Marshal Sir C. Auchinleck, 11 May 1946, Mansergh, op. cit. xii (London, 1983), 800-6.

27 Connell, op. cit. pp.890-3.

28 Note by Field-Marshal Sir C. Auchinleck, 15 August 1947, Mansergh, op. cit. xii, pp.734-7.

29 Connell, op. cit. pp.899-936.

30 See e.g. C. Barnett, *The Desert Generals* (London, 1960); Liddell Hart to Auchinleck, 6 & 20 February 1948, MUL 1308 & 1309.

3

D. F. CORRIGAN
HELEN WADDELL:
Scholar and Author, 1889–1965

D. Felicitas Corrigan, *Helen Waddell: A Biography* (London, 1986) is the sole, authoritative work.

4

K. MC CONKEY
JOHN LAVERY:
Painter, 1856-1941

1 The principal sources of information on the life and work of Sir John Lavery are: Walter Shaw Sparrow, *John Lavery and His Art*, n.d. [1911]. John Lavery, *The Life of a Painter* (London, 1940); Ulster Museum and the Fine Art Society, Sir John Lavery, R.A., 1856-1941, catalogue of an exhibition by Kenneth McConkey, (Belfast, 1984).

5

G. O'BRIEN

CHARLES GAVAN DUFFY:

Rebel and Statesman, 1816–1903

The richest material for Duffy's life may be found in his own *My Life in Two Hemispheres* (2 vols, London, 1898). The first impartial and scholarly account was Leon O Broin's *Charles Gavan Duffy: Patriot and Statesman* (Dublin, 1967). The most recent and highly readable 'life' is Cyril Pearl's *The Three Lives of Gavan Duffy* (New South Wales, 1979). On all of the above the present writer has drawn heavily and gratefully. Specialist studies of events and institutions in which Duffy played a leading role include: Richard Davis, *The Young Ireland Movement* (Dublin, 1986); R. V. Comerford, *The Fenians in Context* — esp. Chap. 1 — (Dublin, 1985); K. B. Nowlan, *The Politics of Repeal* (London, 1965), and the same author's shorter *Charles Gavan Duffy and the Repeal Movement* (Dublin, 1963); J. H. Whyte, *The Independent Irish Party, 1850-9* (Oxford, 1959), and the same author's shorter *The Tenant League and Irish Politics in the Eighteen-Fifties* (Dublin, 1963).

6

R. MC CAUGHEY

JOHN DUNLAP:

Printer, c.1746–1812

1 J. Jackson, 'John Dunlap', *Dictionary of American Biography* (New York, 1930), 3, p.514; A. McClung Lee, 'Dunlap and Claypole: Printers and News-Merchants of the Revolution', *Journalism Quarterly* (1934), 11, 160-178; L. W. Murphy, 'John Dunlap's Packet and its Competitors', *Journalism Quarterly* (1951), 28, 58-62; I. Thomas, *The History of Printing in America* (reprinted New York, 1970); L. C. Wroth, *The Colonial Printer* (reprinted Charlottesville, 1964).

2 E. MacLysaght, *The Surnames of Ireland* (Dublin, 1978), pp.78, 93, 189.

3 Public Record Office of Northern Ireland (P.R.O.N.I.), T.1336/1/25.

4 P.R.O.N.I. T.1336/1/24.

5 P.R.O.N.I. T.1336/1/17.

6 1747 seems the likelier date. The National Trust lists Meetinghouse Street as his birthplace.

7 I. Thomas, op. cit. pp.386-387, 423.

8 A quarter of all titles issued in Lancaster prior to 1770 were for the Presbyterian market. J. H. Wood Jnr, Connestoga Crossroads (Harrisburg, 1979), p.240.

9 I. Thomas, op. cit. p.387.

10 L. C. Wroth, op. cit. p.30.

11 Ibid. pp.133, 149.

12 I. Thomas, op. cit. pp.386-187.

13 Ibid. p.393.

14 A. McClung Lee, op. cit. p.161.

15 Ibid. p.163.

16 L. W. Murphy, op. cit. pp.58, 60.

17 J. Jackson, op. cit. p.515.

18 A. McClung Lee, op. cit. p.167.

19 The first printing of the Declaration of Independence outside America was in the *Belfast News Letter*, 27 August 1776.

20 A. McClung Lee, op. cit. pp.162, 165.

21 Ibid. p.163.

22 L. W. Murphy, op. cit. pp.60-61. It appeared as a daily in 1784.

23 A. McClung Lee, op. cit. pp.170-171.

24 Ibid. p.171.

25 J. M. Coleman, *Thomas McKean — Forgotten Leader of the Revolution* (New Jersey, 1975), p.228. McKean was from Antrim. Dunlap was also

in trouble with Congress in 1779 over some pieces by Thomas Paine published in the *Packet* (A. McClung Lee, op. cit. p.171).

26 P.R.O.N.I. T.1336/1/15. This was in his capacity as one of the first subscribers to the National Bank of the United States.

27 A. McClung Lee, op. cit. p.165.

28 L. W. Murphy, op. cit. p.61. Dunlap took over publication of the Journals until 1785 when the tendering system was introduced.

29 J. H. Campbell, *History of the Friendly Sons of St Patrick and of the Hibernian Society for the Relief of Emigrants from Ireland* (Philadelphia, 1892), pp.109-110.

30 L. W. Murphy, op. cit. p.61.

31 P.R.O.N.I. T.1336/1/15; A. McClung Lee, op. cit. p.163. The 'Whiskey Rebellion' was a series of riots in western Pennsylvania provoked by the government's excise on whiskey.

32 I.D. Rupp, *The History and Topography of Dauphin, Cumberland, Franklin, Bedford, Adams and Perry Counties* (Lancaster, 1846), pp.272-273.

33 P.R.O.N.I. T.1336/1/15.

34 P.R.O.N.I. T.1336/1/18; /21.

35 P.R.O.N.I. T1336/1/14.

36 P.R.O.N.I. T.1336/1/18; 21 (12 May 1785). Dunlap married Mrs Elizabeth Ellison, nee Hayes, of Liverpool.

37 P.R.O.N.I. T.1336/1/20; /22 (May 12, 1785).

38 I. Thomas, op. cit. p.393.

39 J. Jackson, op. cit. p.514.

40 *Cyclopaedia of American Biography* (Ann Arbor, 1967), 19, p.363.

7

S. ICKRINGILL

WILLIAM PATERSON:

Lawyer and Politician, 1745–1806

The best biography of Paterson is John E. O'Connor, *William Paterson* (New Brunswick, 1979). It is still necessary, however, to consult the work of Richard Haskett, particularly for an understanding of Paterson's early career. The best example is Richard Haskett, 'William Paterson, Attorney General of New Jersey: Public Office and Private Profit in the American Revolution'; *William and Mary Quarterly*, 3rd series, 7 (1950). Obviously there is much relevant material on the history of the State of New Jersey. Despite its date of publication, Richard P. McCormick's *Experiment in Independence: New Jersey in the Critical Period 1781-89* (New Brunswick, 1950) is particularly helpful.

Among a considerable amount of primary material, certain collections of manuscript and published printed material should be noted. On the Federal Convention the standard collection is Max Farrand (ed.), *The Records of the Federal Convention* (4 vols, New Haven, 1937). The Paterson Papers in the Library of Congress, the William Paterson Collection in Princeton University Library and the William Paterson Papers in the New Jersey Historical Society all proved to be illuminating.

For those interested in placing Paterson's career in a wider context, the list of reading is enormous. Perhaps the most useful thing to note is the existence of David L. Ammerman and Philip O. Morgan (eds), *Books about Early America: 2001*

Titles (Williamsburg, 1989). Specifically on the question of the early experience of Irish settlers in colonial and early national America, see David N. Doyle, *Ireland, Irishmen and Revolutionary America* (Cork, 1981), Kerby A. *Miller, Emigrants and Exiles: Ireland and the Irish Exodus to North America* (New York, 1985) and Robert J. Dickson, *Ulster Emigration to Colonial America 1718-1775*, with a new Introduction by Graeme E. Kirkham (Belfast, 1988). For an example of a biographical work on one of Paterson's contemporaries with a similar immigrant background to his, see J. Edwin Hendricks *Charles Thomson* (Cranbury, N.J., 1979).

8

A. G. BROWN
JOHN ABERNETHY:
Scholar and Ecclesiast, 1680–1740

1 *Dictionary of National Biography.*

2 J. Duchal, *A Sermon on the Occasion of the Much-Lamented Death of the late Revd Mr John Abernethy* (Belfast, 1741), p.18.

3 Ibid. p.16.

4 Ibid. p.17.

5 Ibid. p.22.

6 J. Abernethy, *The People's Choice, the Lord's Anointed. A Thanksgiving Sermon* (Dublin, 1714).

7 J. Abernethy, *A Sermon Recommending the Study of Scripture-Prophecie*, p.11.

8 Records of the General Synod of Ulster (RGSU) Vol. I, p.69.

9 Ibid. pp.251-3.

10 Ibid. pp.429-30: 458-64: 471-72: 476-77.

11 Ibid. pp.488-89: 492-94: 506.

12 Ibid. pp.523-4: 532-3.

13 This information is based upon a circular letter of the Society dated 7 Dec. 1720 and printed in *A Narrative of the Proceedings of the Seven General Synods*, pp.18ff.

14 Duchal, op. cit. pp.36ff.

15 *A Narrative of the Proceedings of the Seven General Synods*, p.19.

16 Kirkpatrick's conclusion, Duchal, op. cit. p.39.

17 Ibid. p.40.

18 The sermon was published in Belfast in 1720 and is conveniently printed in a volume of Abernethy's works, *Scarce & Valuable Tracts & Sermons*, pp.217ff.

19 Ibid. p.232.

20 Abernethy held that the power of the Apostles in no way constrained the beliefs or conscience of their fellow Christians, but was intended purely to promote truth and sincere religion.

'And from hence we see the just limits of church-power: its decisions bind the conscience as far as men are convinc'd, and no farther; any higher claim of authority not only cannot be inferr'd from the design of ecclesiastical power, according to the scriptures, namely, edification, but indeed is utterly inconsistent with it'. Ibid. pp.246-7.

21 Ibid. pp.252-3.

22 Printed in *Scarce & Valuable Tracts & Sermons*, pp.139ff. The Preface was written by Weld, Choppin and Boyse.

23 Ibid. p.160.

24 Ibid. p.197.

25 Ibid. p.207.

26 Ibid. p.139. Abernethy made the point again when he wrote:

'... but if he means that we have

altered our minds with respect to the doctrines of the Confession it's an unfair insinuation, which common justice will not allow any body to regard until he produces the particular instances wherein we have altered'. Ibid. p.151.

27 He cited Iredell as well as Boyse, Choppin and Weld. Ibid. p.139.

28 Ibid. p.160.

29 Ibid. p.143. The reference is to the Synod in Derry in 1722.

30 Ibid. p.161.

31 *Sermon preached at Antrim on a Fast Day on Account of Divisions*, p.16.

32 Ibid. p.20.

33 Ibid. p.14.

34 Idem.

35 Witherow, op. cit. i, p.197.

36 Published in 1732.

37 The series of five pamphlets was published in 1733. *Reasons for the Repeal of the Sacramental Test*, no. 2.

38 *Printed in Scarce & Valuable Tracts & Sermons*, p.15.

39 Ibid. p.22.

40 Cited in *Scarce & Valuable Tracts and Sermons*, p.276.

41 Ibid. p.277.

42 Ibid. pp.260-61.

43 *Discourses*, vol. II, pp.369-70.

44 This sermon is contained in vol. 4 of the 1751 edition of his sermons, pp.181ff.

45 Ibid. p.193.

46 Ibid. pp.197-199.

47 The Nature and Consequences of the Sac Test Considered in J. Abernethy, *Scarce & Valuable Tracts & Sermons* (London, 1751), pp.78-9.

48 Ibid. p.94.

49 Ibid. pp.95-7: 101-2.

50 Ibid. pp.97-100.

51 Ibid. pp.104-6.

52 Ibid. pp.106-8.

53 Ibid. p.114.

54 Ibid. pp.121ff.

55 Reasons for the Repeal of the Sacramental Test, In Five Numbers, in J. Abernethy, op. cit. pp.63 & 66.

56 Ibid. pp. 69ff.

57 *Dictionary of National Biography.*

58 Mears. *A Sermon on the Occasion of the Much Lamented Death of The Revd Mr John Abernethy* (Dublin 1741), p.48.

59 Idem.

60 Duchal, op. cit. p.24.

61 Mears, op. cit. p.47.

62 Duchal, op. cit. p.18.

63 F.J. Biggar, *The Two Abernethys* (Belfast, 1919), p.10.

64 Ibid. p.8.

65 Witherow, i, p.196.

66 Ibid. p.198.

9

RAYMOND GILLESPIE

OWEN ROE O'NEILL:
Soldier and Politician, c.1582–1649

1 J. T. Gilbert (ed), *A Contemporary History of Affairs in Ireland*, (Dublin, 1879), p.43. This essay cannot hope to be a full biography of Owen Roe but can only give an outline of his life. There are a number of full length biographies of which the most recent is J. I. Casway, *Owen Roe O'Neill and the Struggle for Catholic Ireland* (Philadelphia, 1984).

2 J. I. Casway, 'Owen Roe O'Neill's Return to Ireland in 1642: the Diplomatic Background', *Studia Hibernica*, ix (1969), 48-64.

3 R. Gillespie, 'The End of an Era: Ulster and the Outbreak of the 1641

Rising in C. Brady & R. Gillespie (eds), *Natives and Newcombers: Essays on the Making of Irish Colonial Society 1534-1641* (Dublin, 1986), pp.191-213.

4 J. C. Beckett, 'The Confederation of Kilkenny Reviewed', *Historical Studies*, ii (1959), 29-41, provides an overview of the history of the Confederation.

5 A. Clarke, 'Colonial Identity in Early Seventeenth-Century Ireland' in T. W. Moody (ed), Nationality and the Pursuit of National Independence, *Historical Studies*, xi (Belfast, 1978), pp.57-72; C. Mooney, 'The Irish Sword and the Franciscan Cowl', *Irish Sword*, i (1949), 80-7.

6 Historical Manuscripts Commission, *Report on the Franciscan Manuscripts* (London, 1906), p.134.

7 G. Parker, *The Military Revolution*, (Cambridge, 1988), sets out the main elements of this change.

8 Gilbert, op. cit., i, pp.22-3; Casway, *Owen Roe O'Neill*, pp.84-5.

9 Monsignor Massari, 'My Irish Campaign', *Catholic Bulletin*, vi (1916), 656, vii (1917), 249. For the military background to the army of the Spanish Netherlands, see G. Parker, *The Army of Flanders and the Spanish Road, 1567-1659* (Cambridge, 1972).

10 D. Stevenson, *Scottish Covenanters and Irish Confederates* (Belfast, 1981), pp.103-38; P. O Mordha, 'The Battle of Clones', *Clogher Record*, iv (1962), 148-54.

11 Stevenson, op. cit. pp.139-64.

12 *The Earl of Castlehaven's Review or His Memoirs ... in the Irish Wars* (London, 1684), pp.89-95.

13 Archivo General, Simancas, GA 1566, EO 2523. I am grateful to Jane Ohlmeyer for drawing these references to my attention and for providing me with copies of them.

14 Stevenson, op. cit. pp.220-33; Casway, op. cit. pp.119-36.

15 P. J. Corish, 'Ireland's First Papal Nuncio', *Irish Ecclesiastical Record*, 5th series, lxxxi (1954), 172-83 provides a brief biography.

16 Casway, op. cit. pp.144.

17 *Calendar of State Papers, Ireland, 1608-10*, p.195.

18 Ibid. 1603-6, pp.396-8; 1608-10, p.62.

19 B. Jennings (ed), *Wild Geese in Spanish Flanders* (Dublin, 1964), pp.259, 494.

20 Gilbert, op. cit., i, pp.396-7.

21 *Calendar of Carew Manuscripts*, 1601-3, pp.50-1.

22 This community has been well dealt with in G. Henry, 'Wild Geese in Spanish Flanders: the Irish Military Community in Flanders 1586-1610, an Emerging Identity,' M.A. thesis, St. Patrick's College, Maynooth, 1986.

23 Jennings, op. cit. pp.230-1.

24 Ibid. p.214.

25 Archivo General, Simancas, EO 2523.

26 Historical Manuscripts Commission, *Report on the Salisbury Manuscripts* (London, 1915), xviii, pp.62-3.

27 Edmund Hogan (ed.), *A History of the Wars in Ireland* (Dublin, 1873), p.48.

28 Massari, 'My Irish Campaign', *Catholic Bulletin*, vi (1916), 369; J. Bossy, 'Catholicity and Nationalism in the Northern Counter Reformation' in St Mews (ed), *Religion and National Identity: Studies in Church History*, xviii (Oxford, 1982), pp.285-96.

29 Massari, op. cit. pp.479, 480, 503; vi (1916), p.503.

30 Cal. S. P. Ire., 1606-8, p.415; Massari, op. cit., pp.536, 583-4.

31 The state of the Counter Reformation in Ireland is well summed up in J. Bossy, 'The Counter Reformation and the people of Catholic Ireland', *Historical Studies* viii, (Dublin, 1971), pp.155-159.

32 A. Hutton (ed), *The Embassy in Ireland of Mgr G. B. Rinuccini* (Dublin, 1873), p.53.

33 P. J. Corish, 'Rinuccini's Censure of May 22, 1648, *Irish Theological Quarterly*, xviii (1951), 322-37; 'The Crisis in Ireland in 1648: The Nuncio and the Supreme Council: Conclusions', *Irish Theological Quarterly*, xxii (1955), 231-57.

34 Casway, op. cit., pp.192-4, 210.

35 P. J. Corish, 'John Callaghan and the controversies among the Irish in Paris, 1648-54', *Irish Theological Quarterly*, xxi (1954), 32-50.

36 C. O'Rahilly (ed.) *Five Seventeenth-Century Political Poems* (Dublin, 1952), pp.23-7.